LATINO BUSINESSPERSON IN SILICON VALLEY

An Inspirational Account of an Experience as an Entrepreneur

No part of this book can be transmitted or reproduced in any form, including print, electronic, photocopying, scanning, mechanical, or recording without prior written permission from the author.

This is a work of creative nonfiction, with a presentation of events to the best of the author's intuition and experience. While all the information in this book is true, some names and identifying details have been changed to protect the privacy of the people involved.

This book has been written for information purposes only, and every effort has been made to make it as complete and accurate as possible. However, there may be mistakes in typography or content. Also, since the information herein extends only up to the publishing date, by necessity information about the author's life since that time is not included.

The author's purpose is to inspire and motivate minorities to get out of their comfort zones and show the world what they are capable of achieving, regardless of their ethnicities. The author and the publisher do not warrant that the information contained in this book is fully complete and shall not be responsible for any errors or omissions. The author and publisher shall have neither liability nor responsibility to any person or entity concerning any loss or damage caused or alleged to be caused directly or indirectly by this book.

TABLE OF CONTENTS

ABOUT THE AUTHOR

Sergio Retamal is the CEO of Global4PL, a supply chain operation and consulting services company that helps companies boost their sales and meet compliance goals as well as reach their full operational potential. Global4PL deals in customs brokerage, technology solutions, IOR-EOR services, and supply chain consulting with firms operating in more than 164 countries. Sergio is also a co-founder of DPLGuru, an online software solution that handles US import/export law compliance.

Sergio completed his Bachelor of Science in International Business as well as his MBA in International Business from California State University, Northridge. He holds a Master's degree in Organizational Development (MSOD) from Pepperdine University's Graziadio Business School.

Sergio's professional career spans more than 25 years in procurement and supply chain organizations and operations. Before launching Global4PL and DPLGuru, he took on various management roles in the US, Latin America, Europe, and Asia. Some of these roles included planning and leading global supply chain strategies for companies such as Micropolis, Cost Plus, Ryder Integrated Logistics, and Sun Microsystems. He directs the development and management for complete supply chain networks, managing logistics and import/export teams in both small and large established organizations.

Sergio has not only led logistics at several Fortune 100 companies, but he also taught logistics in the California State University system. He is acclaimed as a leader in supply chain and logistics.

His determination and experience have earned him several awards, including mentions in *The Supply & Demand Chain Executive Magazine*, where his name appeared in the 'Top Pros-to-Know' list an unprecedented 13 times. In 2005, the International

Transportation Association awarded Sergio with the 'Executive of the Year' award, which is a significant achievement in the industry. Previous recipients of this award include Wal-Mart's senior vice president, Bruce T. Peterson, the governor of the state of Delaware, Thomas R. Carper, and the chairman of David Oppenheimer Group of Companies, Gary Hammonds.

At a ceremony in Washington D.C, Sergio's unmatched contributions earned the company the President's E award for incredible export services. This award is the highest recognition any US entity can receive for contributions to the expansion of US exports. It was introduced by President Kennedy in a 1961 executive order following World War II to honor and provide recognition to America's best performing exporters.

Global4PL was also the first company to receive the 'Exporter of the Year 2018 Award' from American Express, The company appears on the cover of industry magazines and has won other industry-specific awards based on customer satisfaction and performance case studies. Indeed, Global4PL has more awards and recognitions than any 4PL/IOR company in the industry.

Sergio Retamal is the chair of the board of directors for the Latino Foundation of Silicon Valley. The group is dedicated to inspiring community philanthropy and engaging people to invest in the educational excellence and leadership development of young Latinos while convening and engaging the Latino community to improve the quality of life for Latinos and the Silicon Valley region.

Mr. Retamal is also a San Francisco Federal Reserve Bank Economic Advisory Member. The Twelfth District Economic Advisory Council is a source of information on current and pending economic developments in the Twelfth District. The members, all of whom reside within the nine-state district, provide observations, opinions, and advice to members of the boards of directors and management of the Federal Reserve Bank of San Francisco.

PREFACE

Writing this book was like putting together a puzzle with no picture to serve as a guide. Since the beginning, Mr. Retamal knew what this book was going to be about, but was lost on what aspects of his life should be included and what should be omitted.

Simply put, this book is an account of his life as an entrepreneur in Silicon Valley and how to succeed as a young Latino in the valley. It includes advice regarding diversifying the valley, especially at executive levels. Sergio recognizes that had he been an American white male, things would have been a lot easier. In time, he realized what a difference it made to be a Latino in the valley.

Regardless of everything he faced, he believes that whatever he is today is a result of all those challenges and hardships, and more than anything else, the inspiration from his mother. She's the one who urged him to own a startup in an arena as dynamic as Silicon Valley. She was a mother who would take up any challenge that lay ahead of her. She certainly knew how to feed and nurture five children alone.

In writing this book, he has made use of some of his personal experiences in Silicon Valley to highlight his observations and the decisions he made in building his business. These experiences helped him understand how to lead life instead of simply living it. There was a time when he would just wait for a lucky break, but then he realized the importance of creating opportunities for himself. From that point on, he took the challenge to turn things around instead of bending to the status quo. That's when he began to disown professional imprisonment and turn it to his advantage. The rest of his life was all about recognizing opportunities, innovation, and action. He believes that every young Latino can follow his lead and build.

Most importantly, he recognizes that all the data presented by the government organizations about the Latino community hardly capture the intricacies present in real life. While moving through his entrepreneurial journey, he tries to do justice to the Latino community by highlighting the real challenges they face in the corporate world. He initially aimed to keep this book strictly professional but soon recognized that the strong correlation between the community's social status and the career opportunities available to them cannot be ignored.

One of the initial considerations in writing this book was to have a clear vision of who should benefit from reading it. This book primarily seeks to inspire minorities to believe in themselves and refuse to accept defeat. It serves as a valuable guide to Latinos in the US. If a Latino/a can make his or her way to the top in Silicon Valley, he or she can grow in every other market in the world. So, if you're a Latino/a living in the US, try to make the most of this book to prepare yourself for what lies ahead.

Community social work scholars and practitioners will also find this book useful. They will uncover insights about racial and ethnic issues in business with a focus on the Latino community, allowing them to enter uncharted areas. This book will enrich an awareness that has just begun in the valley, and at the same time build an understanding of existing Latino support systems and encourage corporations to increase their support.

Upon completion of this book, Sergio is pleased with the accomplishment and enjoying the final picture of his life puzzle. He truly hopes that you enjoy reading this book. If you view things from his perspective, you won't stop reading.

THE JOURNEY

Sergio was born in Chile, and his family moved to the US when he was five months old. A lawyer and one of the youngest mayors in Chile, his father was invited to Washington, DC, for a worldwide symposium for mayors in Washington. There, the young man visited the White House and fell in love with the US. After this trip, he decided to shift the entire family to California. Sergio's mother was a full-time caretaker of five children. It was quite the shock for her; from being the wife of a lawyer and the mayor to living in Watts, California, a few miles south of Los Angeles. Prone to riots, Watts was not the greatest of cities for Latino immigrants.

Sergio's father did not speak English and was no longer a licensed attorney in this country so he took all kinds of jobs to make ends meet. He worked as a taxi driver, a photographer, and a door-to-door salesperson in the California Latino community. Sergio's mother helped by doing laundry and ironing for the neighbors. Living in Watts was extremely difficult. Eventually, these difficulties, combined with other negative experiences, led to the couple's divorce.

After the divorce, Sergio and his siblings moved back to Chile with their mother. Sergio couldn't speak Spanish, so he was deprived of initial schooling. He also lost his first language, because he hardly spoke English while back in his native land.

Sergio came back to the US when he was 24 years old to stay for good. While living in Chile, he had some great experiences that helped him transform into the person that he is today. Chile is a great country with great people, but it had its share of political and natural disasters during the years that the family lived there, from the first Communist – Leninist government elected democratically, to a coup organized by the CIA, to earthquakes from 8.5 to 8.8. Nevertheless, events come and go, and Sergio learned how to make the best out of situations, no matter how critical.

Life can be bizarre at times and when Sergio thinks of the past now, it gives him goosebumps. For example, in 1973, Chile faced a coup that had a dramatic effect on his life. Some Communists entered his city and hid in a hospital. The military decided to attack them and the building was going to be bombed by the Air Force. Unfortunately, Sergio's family house was only two blocks from the hospital. No bomb was ever dropped, but the stress the insurgency created between the military and the Communists was immense.

More important, there was a busy maternity clinic nearby. He can recall that many women who were headed to it for deliveries hid between the trees to avoid being shot by either side, stuck between life and death, not able to reach the clinic that day. Despite being only nine years old, Sergio was courageous enough to bring some of those women to his home and do whatever he could to help calm them down. One of the women was in labor, and he will never forget the tension associated with dealing with her. Somehow, the family managed to keep control of the situation until the next morning, when all the women were safely moved to the hospital.

This was the first major stress test in his life. It toughened him as a person and prepared him for everything that lay ahead. It proved to him that he could face adversity, and he had what it takes to handle tough situations. It prepared him for the pitfalls of trying to start a business in Silicon Valley. He was exposed to shooting, deprivation, uncertainty, and other horrific events well before he tried to make it on his own. Such events can easily cause psychological strains on any young child, but he took everything positively and used the events to his benefit.

REASONS TO LAUNCH A STARTUP

After Sergio's mother instilled in him the desire to have his own business, he became inspired. He had seen the hardships his mother had gone through, starting from odd jobs to supplying bricks for launching a small construction business with her brother. This inspiration translated into several other reasons to launch a business of his own.

He either inherited creativity from his mother or learned it from her experiences and struggles. It was a sense of legacy, but even before he stepped into his professional life, he had enjoyed creating and organizing things. It gave him a sense of achievement to set up projects from scratch and nurture them to new heights. The desire expanded into the aspiration for entrepreneurship—the idea of starting a venture, an organization that had a purpose and goal.

His entrepreneurial ambitions were strengthened by the satisfying idea of creating jobs. He had seen the hardships his mother had gone through and experienced the struggles himself. All too aware of what it felt like to be discriminated against and unemployed, he didn't want others to go through the same ordeal. This was a way to create jobs for people and for himself.

Furthermore, what boosted him was the continuous glass ceiling or "unconscious bias" for Latinos. Plainly speaking, some very subtle and not so subtle racist experiences created in him a need to not just break the glass ceiling but rather remove it altogether. He wanted to make a path for Latinos to rise through the ranks with less struggle. Luckily, the different forms of discrimination he had faced worked to his benefit. As they say, what doesn't kill you makes you stronger.

That's exactly how he had responded each time he faced any kind of discrimination during the early part of his professional career. Instead of being threatened by racial discrimination and deprivations, he increased the pace of his professional growth. He remained professional and it served him throughout his career. Rather than taking his ethnicity as a weakness, he used all those negative experiences to feed his desire to become better and stronger. He knew he wanted to do something big and let everyone know what he was capable of. His ultimate aim in life became to prove himself as a world-class entrepreneur, launching a business from scratch then growing it to a global level. As his mother had before him, he persevered through it all, using the strength he had both witnessed and built throughout his life. He never gave up, and he hopes Latinos do the same and genuinely earn and live the title "up and coming."

LATINO BUSINESSPERSON IN SILICON VALLEY

An Inspirational Account of an Experience as an Entrepreneur

CHAPTER ONE

WHY HE CHOSE SILICON VALLEY

Silicon Valley is largely recognized as the breeding ground for technology startups. A great many of the major tech giants such as Apple, HP, Adobe, Google, Intel, eBay, etc, are located there, operating with continued business success. Not only does the region attract local startups, but international tech-entrepreneurs also aim to get a footprint there. The following are the primary reasons Sergio chose Silicon Valley for his launch.

SILICON VALLEY IS AS AMERICAN AS APPLE PIE

What makes Silicon Valley unique is that it's a utopia for most entrepreneurs. You won't find an environment like it anywhere else in the world. Silicon Valley is the land where riches are made, and the latest technologies are developed. It is a place for giants and dreamers. The "flow" is multidimensional: a talented and achievement-oriented workforce; well-connected minds from Stanford University and the University of California Berkeley, as well as many other top universities; and leaders whose entrepreneurial spirit sparks "Unicorn fever." (A "Unicorn" is a privately held startup company with a value of over $1 billion.)

As Google's chief Internet evangelist, Vint Cerf, describes it: there are well-trained marketers, engineers, researchers, and businesses; a dynamic venture capital community; experienced businessmen to guide startups; and the supportive California law. When you consider all these aspects collectively, it becomes easy to see how new (white male) ventures can thrive in Silicon Valley. With the help of CEOs such as Sergio, hopefully, this land of opportunity will open itself up to more than just white males.

THE LAND OF FAILURE IS A BADGE OF HONOR

Unlike most other regions that do not value startups, Silicon Valley provides the required motivational framework important for tech startups. It revolves around the key entrepreneurship values of innovation, risk-taking, and collaboration. You might be able to obtain financial assistance around Wall Street, but you won't be able to seek insights into launching and managing tech startups, learn about technological innovation or obtain the level of expertise you'd achieve in Silicon Valley.

Sergio was determined to keep learning from his surroundings and expand his professional network. Silicon Valley was a great place to find and connect with supportive and experienced mentors belonging to the technological field, and seek their guidance to take his new venture forward. It seemed to be a perfect location for his business. He worked tirelessly to collaborate and network to find the right help to get ahead in this environment.

STRENGTH OF COLLABORATION

Collaboration in Silicon Valley is the root of success. Building positive connections through networking is the foundation of a successful company. Learning how to make and maintain these connections will support the life of a business.

A college degree helps in being successful in Silicon Valley, but it is not always necessary. College will give you access to a network of individuals with a good statistical chance to succeed, both from a professional and personal networking point of view.

However, If you did not have a chance to go to college, you need to know what type of network you need to support you both personally and in business for the long term. Get involved with the Chamber of Commerce, go to Small Business Administration events, search for college extension programs that offer single courses for a discounted fee, sign up for professional associations and attend events. Events include trade magazine events, non-profit meetups, business journal events, church events, community events, and more. Use as many avenues as possible to talk about your business and network with others in your industry. Additionally, reach out to collaborate with other businesses, and they will return the favor.

Collaborating with other businesses is typically done through networking. You need to find people in your area or industry that can benefit from you either as a client, as a connector or as a service provider. You need to surround yourself with people and companies that are looking to lift all boats and help each other. By default, if you offer help to others, you will receive help in return.

It's important to remember that this takes time, but also an understanding that both companies will benefit from the relationship. Sergio recalls plenty of instances of companies that look for more in return than they give; these relationships don't last long and benefit no one. Approach companies with the intent of helping and building a long term business relationship.

Develop a strategy for approaching other businesses. As you are starting as a small company, look for others who have services or products you need so you can strategically source those services from them, building a relationship. After the relationship is established, take the time to introduce yourself, your company, and how your company will serve them. This requires time and the maturity to know that just because you buy from them doesn't mean they must buy from you. Remember that people like to buy from people they like or know, so you will have a better chance at getting a sale from them when they know you better.

Getting to know the other company also takes time. Remember that they are as busy as you, so the relationship may take more time to build. However, human beings like to reciprocate, so if you spend time helping others and promoting others, they will reciprocate. Learn about businesses in your neighborhood and city, perhaps at Chamber of Commerce meetings, or by shopping local, or at any other business meeting, and spread the word. Two things will happen when you start talking more about fellow businesses. People will appreciate that you are helping them with a good reference, and the people referred by you will most likely take the time to appreciate it by getting to know you. Some will even return the favor and refer your business. Most networkers are skilled at connecting people without expecting something in return, but normally karma works in their favor, and word of mouth business grows.

Developing the necessary networking skills is all about listening and learning about the other company or person. People like to be heard and understood, but not sold. This means that you need to take the time to listen to your customers or fellow business owners, pay attention to their needs, study their websites and follow their social media announcements. You can't help someone unless you know what they need and you can't target something if you don't know what you are pursuing.

Organizations such as the MBE Certification Organization focus on helping minorities grow and work with large companies, including providing networking and collaboration opportunities. However, this process takes time, and you have to be patient as well as willing to spend a lot of time on the process, which may take months or years, with no guarantees

It becomes easy to find synergies for common goals when similar businesses are located nearby. Lobbying as a combined industry creates a joint industry strength with many benefits. For instance, high-tech businesses in Silicon Valley can pressure the government to raise the cap on foreign employee visas, share common service providers such as transport or food for employees, request a dedicated transportation service from a particular suburb, and so on.

THE DREAM OF FINANCING

Even though you need a significant amount of investment to launch a company in Silicon Valley, it has established itself as an ideal location for funding great business ideas for most people. The region comprises a high amount of personal and institutional wealth, and there exist thousands of venture capitalists and angel investors looking for investment opportunities instead of paying high taxes on their businesses. They're determined to pour funds into a diversified portfolio of businesses to earn dividends.

Although most startups do fail in Silicon Valley, the high number of startups means that there will be one or two success stories from every lot. Further, a businessperson who fails once has ample opportunity to try again, as long as he or she has maintained positive integrity. By investing in a diverse portfolio of businesses, investors reduce their risks. For those who are denied funding by dozens of investors, there are hundreds more to whom they can pitch their ideas.

If a business idea is exciting, it is easy to attract venture capitalists. While pitching unique business ideas is crucial to get the buy-in from financiers, you still need a high level of networking among capitalists to secure the funding. This is when organizations such as the MBE Certification Organization come into play.

What's even more tempting about the investors in Silicon Valley is that the majority of them are willing to offer a tremendous degree of support, guidance, connections, and mentorship over and above the financial support. You need to think beyond the financial lines when you decide to align with an investor. Remember to continuously network for future collaboration; these are the companies that open doors for you.

Financing opportunities was one of the reasons Sergio considered Silicon Valley. However, all his expectations were proved wrong when he later found that raising finance can be a big setback if you're a Latino or any other class that is not a white male. This is where he aims to raise awareness and make changes within the valley.

PAST SUCCESS STORIES MAKE A BIG DIFFERENCE

The possibility of business success in Silicon Valley is strongly linked to the incredible success stories from the past. For both investors and entrepreneurs, there's something about being surrounded by the best corporations that make it easier to remain optimistic and imagine victories for your business.

Keeping diversity issues aside, there exists a sort of brotherhood in the region that commends the next generation to achieve greatness. While spending time in Silicon Valley, you will keep hearing unique experiences, incredible war stories, and case studies that will inspire you to dream big, innovate and succeed.

Sergio and his business are an example of success, with an extra layer. He is a Latino who made it in a place built for the white male. He believes that if he made his dreams possible, you can do it, too.

UNIQUE APPROACH TO FAILURE

In Silicon Valley, you not only learn from past success stories but also past failures. Despite all the positives, numerous businesses fail in Silicon Valley. Recently, a survey was conducted with 50 entrepreneurs from Silicon Valley to uncover the secrets of success in the region. The results disclosed that entrepreneurs had a level-headed approach to failures. Despite failures, their day-to-day determination is unsurpassed elsewhere. This is largely due to the ability to try again after a failure.

Silicon Valley businessmen are typically comfortable with failing experiments. Instead of letting themselves down, they take the challenge to assess, refine and re-introduce the failed system to make it work. It was because of this culture that Sergio was able to keep up his spirits when his initial software launch didn't work. He will discuss this later in the book.

One amazing principle he learned from working in Silicon Valley is that a business idea, in itself is important, but the key is the idea's refinement and strategic execution that paves the way for success.

Businesses rely on the mantra 'fail fast' as opposed to the rest of the world that doesn't want to fail. This gives Silicon Valley an edge, especially for startups. What these businesses know is that you learn a lot more from failures than temporary success and victories. A failure is only a failure if you do not learn from it and if you don't try again.

TIPS FOR STANDING OUT

Standing out among all the other talents here is not easy, more so for Latinos, as we culturally tend to shy away from being in the spotlight. We are often taught to not brag, instead of letting our results speak for themselves. Shying away from the spotlight will hurt you because in Silicon Valley you must stand out to get noticed among investors and customers alike. In fact, you are selling yourself. You are the product. If you want the product to be bought by investors, the public, then you must sell yourself, your company, and your idea as a professional without overselling or being misleading.

There are ways to get noticed in Silicon Valley, even though Latinos have to work harder for it. When someone asks for a volunteer to lead a project, be the first to raise your hand. When you have an opportunity to stretch your scope of knowledge, take it and learn from it. When there is a request for nominations for awards or new opportunities, nominate yourself or ask someone else that knows your worth to nominate you. Remember, once you get an award, chances are that you could get it again because you've established a track record for receiving it.

Nominating themselves is something most people don't do. However, there will be a few times that you will be the only nominee. This happens often with scholarships, awards, promotions, and more. Sometimes, you're lucky enough to stand alone, and win an award that you can use in your portfolio for future clients.

Luck is a combination of hard work, being in the right place at the right time, and looking for opportunities. You have to try as much as possible to make your own opportunities, which others will see as good luck. Good luck seldom falls in those who are not prepared or looking for an opportunity.

If you do fail in your first business venture, if you have not developed a new technology, or if you have not received other types of funding, you will learn fast, that Silicon Valley is an expensive place to live. There is the myth of the area, then the reality that you have to be in the right place, at the right time, with the right business, and know the right people. However, what most people will experience is a land of well-educated, motivated, and driven people that want to be part of the dream. This will motivate you to keep trying. Just like most people, that motivation has made Silicon Valley the tiny start of the business world and just like the lottery, only a few people hit the jackpot, but that dream is what keeps all of them going.

CHAPTER TWO

LAUNCHING A STARTUP

It is recommended to continue to work for others while trying to launch a startup business. It is important to remember that revenue and all expenses for the first six months, most likely will not come from the startup itself. There must be additional income from somewhere to cover this. Working on the business after hours or holding a part-time job will help you survive rather than starting with the risk of running out of money. There are many part-time jobs or gigs that will ensure you an income until your company is able to produce enough to pay you and your employees. Try to get part-time or gig work that is related to your desired industry; if that's not possible, do whatever it takes to maintain an income.

TRANSITIONING TO WORKING FOR YOURSELF

The transition from working for someone else to working for yourself is difficult on two levels. When you start your own business, you are giving yourself a salary, as well as all benefits, such as health insurance, that an established company would give you. When the economy is not so good, the larger companies will be able to weather the storm better. A small business may not do so well.

The second level is the mental component. When you're working for a company you work five or six days a week, you're responsible to perform your job and the corporation is responsible for everything else. You have the limited scope of an employee with one job, rather than the encompassing scope of the business owner, who has full ownership for every function within the company. If something is not going well, it falls on the business owner to ensure that it gets fixed.

Additionally, when you work for yourself you are working seven days a week. You need to ensure that everything is working properly. You are responsible for all functions, and many times you are the person who comes in early, and then stays late. If any area, from sales, to marketing, to purchasing or shipping, is not working correctly, it is up to you to jump in and fix it or find an external solution to the problem.

This means that a small company owner, such as yourself, holds all the weight of the company. Not only do you have your own job to perform, but you also have the whole weight of the corporation on your shoulders. This includes all departments, employees, interactions, finances, and more. At times, this is a heavy burden. You may find that you have to pay your employees and not yourself, or that you aren't finding the right solutions or some other issue that makes the job heavy on you. However, despite these weights, the reward of starting a business is the independence you have in decision-making and leading your own company. You are the boss, you make the rules according to how you feel it should be done.

The rule of thumb for transitioning from working for someone to working for yourself is that you should be able to support yourself without revenue for six to twelve months if you are a business to business (B2B). Note that most companies will pay net45 which might mean net90 or more on your first few invoices as you will be a new vendor to them and companies are in no hurry to pay vendors, no matter how badly you need the money. Net45 is an invoicing term that means a company has 45 days to make the payment from the time their accounting department receives the invoice.

STARTUP FUNDS

Finding startup funds is a bigger challenge for a young Latino than it is for others. In Sergio's case, he used money he had saved from his corporate job to help with startup costs. Using savings or loans from friends and family is typically the best way to get necessary startup funds, as loans are normally not feasible for the first few months or years in most cases. Investors are also a limited option, as discussed before. They do have pitfalls, however, which will be discussed later. The truth is that most Latino startups rely on personal loans and finances.

The most important thing to do, as a startup, is to prepare a budget and understand your own access to cash and loans prior to launching the company, as well as building a credit score. You might hear about easy loans, but the fact is that banks are typically not the best source for a business with no history of profits to show. It will take a few years to gain enough capital to prove to a bank that your company is worthy of a loan. Further, banks will not touch you if you have a poor credit score, or have not been in business for at least five years. They want a return on their investment in you, and they want to know for sure they will get their money back.

Having a good credit score gives you access to bigger solutions, such as Sergio's solution to funding a large project. This project required his company to pay $200,000 a month to vendors for over 18 months total. He was able to charge the expense to his corporate credit card and move the project forward. Without good credit, this project would have not been able to launch. Moreover, his positive credit score and card usage granted him access to better programs set up for businesses, specifically a program that gave him a line of credit based on the company's credit score merits, called the "working capital terms." This allowed him to tackle larger expenditures to gain better-established vendors. There are many companies that provide services to businesses that work to build good credit scores over time.

CHALLENGES FOR YOUNG LATINOS

There are many challenges for young Latinos in Silicon Valley outside of race discrimination, which will be discussed later. Many Latinos in this position may be the first person in their family to go to college or start a business, so they most likely won't have others in their family to serve as a mentor. This is why it is essential for young Latino business owners hopefuls to network and get a mentor as soon as possible. A mentor will provide unbiased advice and will listen to the young person's ideas.

It is essential for young Latinos to start developing their networks. To work with their mentors, and get close to others with similar experiences, to be able to survive in the first five years of business. As a Latino, you must remember that the cards are stacked against you, and your success will be borrowed from the success of others. There is a lack of access and resources for you, so networking and getting to know others who have gone before you is your best path to success. While some of you will be lucky enough to find investors, many of you will need to rely on networking and personal funds in the beginning.

CHAPTER THREE

THE LAUNCH

LIFELONG PREPARATION

Since the beginning, Sergio knew that he would have his own business someday. From a young age, he was interested in the supply chain but as his corporate exposure increased, he realized how fast technology was taking over the industry.

To develop his understanding and prepare himself for the industry, he enrolled at California State University for his MBA, and later on, he went to Graziadio Business School to pursue his Master's in Organizational Development (MSOD).

The MSOD turned out to be a truly fantastic program and he was glad he enrolled in it. It was focused on developing people skills, which are also called "soft skills." It turned out to be an ideal program for future managers, business leaders, and consultants who wish to learn soft skills. Soft skills are crucial to managing teams and individuals in organizations. Besides helping him recognize his strengths and weaknesses, the program turned him into a better consultant, a better manager, and a better person because as a consultant, you aren't just concerned about your business interests, you also help clients resolve their issues and help them achieve success.

However, helping other companies isn't simple either, especially when it comes to pointing out what they're doing wrong. The MSOD program also taught him how to handle such cases. Pinpointing issues to people can be a challenge, more so when they are part of the issue. Among the most daunting tasks is to truthfully tell people that their ego is affecting their efficiency.

Likewise, when high-profile executives are involved, consultants are often influenced by their status and won't disclose complete truths. Others will tell them what they want to hear. Being truthful though comes with its own consequences. You may find yourself at fault for trying to be honest. For instance, you might be told that you're trying to hide your faults by raising the company's problems.

To handle such cases, you need soft skills that are acquired through education, work experience, and possessing technical knowledge. Some of the most important soft skills a business owner should have include: empathy, team building, communication, listening to others, and self-awareness, which includes one's ego and how our behavior affects others.

Empathy is crucial, as management is about people and understanding others, including customers, employees, and vendors. This is a key factor to getting to the core of people, finding out what they need, and asking them to believe in your vision. You need to understand what that means to other people, how it makes them feel, and how it motivates them. Without empathy, your ability to manage people and incite motivation within them is almost impossible.

Team building, which is an overused word, is not about just getting things done. It is also about what you, as a business owner and CEO, do to set up systems, roles, and responsibilities within your team. It's about building culture, rewards, and accountability.

Some may call this "culture," but company culture builds over time. In the beginning, it is better to call this "team-building."

Communication means listening more than speaking. A business owner relies on motivation to succeed and to create something that allows him or her to take the risk of starting a business. Sometimes this passion is so strong that the business owner believes he or she is right and knows better than seasoned businessmen, women, or mentors. This belief, which is sometimes a self-defense mechanism, consequently disregards other's opinions and views that don't align with the new business's vision. As the business grows larger, this narrow vision will affect others working in the company. This is called the Halo Effect. The CEO asserts his or her beliefs on the company, leaving the employees to believe that their opinions don't matter. This is no way to run a company.

This is why communication is more about listening and about accepting feedback than it is about giving orders. Everyone must have informed views before making decisions, including company owners. If you create an environment where people are afraid of you or don't feel their feedback would be welcome, you damage your organization. If your employees don't feel comfortable approaching you with feedback or ideas, will fellow businesses also view you as unapproachable? Listening to both the employees and fellow business owners keeps your network healthy, and it helps you solve company problems. You want information from people closest to the problem that you're trying to solve; you want to know how you can help your extended business network partners. Do not dismiss feedback, build a reputation of listening and hearing what others have to say.

If you are questioning your communication skills, set up a system to provide yourself with feedback from people who are paid for this type of service. Consultant companies are ready to assess your company to find problems and deliver solutions. If you don't set up the mechanism, you won't get the benefit of timely, productive, and realistic feedback.

CEO Roundtables are another smart avenue to receive feedback. Here, you can exchange ideas with people who have nothing to lose if they tell you the truth. They are more likely to help you find issues within your company because they don't feel any risk in approaching you.

Finally, utilize informal communication. There are many people who either hate to ask questions or are too intimidated to talk to executives because they don't see the benefit of risking their job, or they simply don't like the attention. For example, Sergio has found that some people do not find him approachable for a range of reasons. Because of this, he asks for feedback from those who he knows have no problem providing it. These people gather the responses from those who may find Sergio unapproachable, ensuring every voice is heard. He validates the observations and assessments his employees have made, lets people know that they are heard, and acts on what needs to be done. If he did not have an informal feedback channel, he would miss important information from those closest to the problem. He uses many different avenues to gather the responses to ensure he hears as many voices as possible.

Self-awareness is a skill that must be worked on all the time. Ego and the inner self are part of you, which makes them impossible to see unless you use a strong reality mirror. You must always analyze how you are acting and the effect your actions have on your business and on the people around you. If you don't stop to smell the roses, you will not know if you're looking at roses or durians. The durian is a banned fruit in Asian countries due to its pungent smell. It does not know it smells bad; it just keeps going in life. However, others do notice it. When you don't stop to assess your behavior and how it is affecting your business, you start to smell. Soon, you will be banned from the network you worked so hard to build. Hence, always remember to assess and reassess often to maintain positive business relationships.

Learning, perfecting, and improving these soft skills requires preparation and practice. You may study concepts such as organizational development, psychology, take classes in dealing with people, work on negotiation tactics, and more to develop your soft skills. You must care about them as much as you care about anything else for your business. Make them a part of your personal training, and revisit them to make sure they stay fresh.

After college and developing his soft skills, Sergio tried hard to find a job in the logistics and supply chain industry. He had a manager position for a 24-Hour Alarm company that paid a good salary. He chose to forfeit the earnings when he got an offer from a computer manufacturing company to serve as an export coordinator. It paid 30% less than the manager's job, yet he chose to accept the offer as it provided him a tremendous opportunity to break into the industry. This decision helped him start networking and got him into the right industry to move forward with his business. If an opportunity such as this presents itself, calculate the risk and take it, if you can.

From here, Sergio worked his way up the industry, spending 20 years serving in several US-based companies with worldwide distribution networks and manufacturing facilities in Asia. While serving in those companies, he traveled extensively to Asia, Europe, and Latin America.

Since the very start, he kept his eyes open for constant learning opportunities. This was the reason he kept on taking every opportunity he got, working on different supply chain roles to diversify his skills and learn about all areas of the field. He was gathering not only valuable contacts but information about the inner workings of the industry.

Plus, he knew the importance of developing a network so wherever he went around the world, he was meeting professionals from the industry and building relationships to broaden his network. Those networking efforts paid off. When he finally launched his business in 2004, he was able to expand his clientele beyond the US, working with more than 168 countries today.

If Sergio had to sum up all his pre-startup experiences in a few words, he'd say that it gave him the capacity to handle uncertainty and complex situations with ease.

THE BUSINESS IDEA AND LAUNCH

Based on his academic and professional experiences, Sergio decided to launch a supply chain software tool to serve the small and large organizations in Silicon Valley. It was developed, and he tried to approach clients but no one wanted to be the first one to buy the new product. Moreover, why would people rely on a software tool developed by a Latino? He'll talk about the lack of cultural diversity in Silicon Valley later in the book but he believes that one of the reasons why this product failed was because of his Latino origin.

The software idea didn't work out so he prepared to drop the idea completely. He approached his university to seek consultancy and feedback from MBA students on what they thought about the software. They opened his eyes. They candidly told him that his company was more of a software consultancy company rather than a software company, which is supposed to be something huge, especially when it came to operating in Silicon Valley. Using this alternative avenue gave him answers he could not find amongst his colleagues.

He began to think that a consultancy business was not a bad idea. Without giving it a second thought, he decided to go for it. He chose to be much more research-oriented this time. In addition to relying on the insightful recommendations given by the university students, he adopted a customer-driven approach. He diverted his focus on what the customers need.

Once he uncovered market insights, he went on to work on his supply chain consultancy software, which was self-funded. He soon learned that when you're a Latino, or belong to any other minority group, attracting an investor is next to impossible, even in Silicon Valley where investors are looking for opportunities to invest. While the atmosphere and drive to succeed are positive, the reality of finding an investor is different. As mentioned before, there are plenty of investors in the valley, but many of them look for business owners who look like them or graduated from the same university as them. This puts Latinos in a tougher spot. Eventually, Sergio relied on self-funding and launched his business with a team of two employees.

CHAPTER FOUR

STAGES OF DEVELOPMENT

THE FIRST YEAR

As you should expect, the first year in business is always difficult. Not only do you need to create everything your business needs to perform whatever service or product you offer, but you must make sales as well. To sell, you need to set up the business from the website to the marketing materials, to the sales pitch. You need to start networking before the business is launched, and you need to start working with many different vendors. You may need a website designer, an accountant, a supplier, and more before you open the front doors. Even with the best preparation, your first business attempt might fail. Remember that failure only means a chance to learn and try again. However, many businesses that fail in the first year rise from the ashes and build something successful. Keep networking, keep attending conferences, and keep talking to people about your business to help it succeed. Remind people you still exist with monthly communications and website updates. Recommend other businesses to friends and family, so the business owners will return the favor and recommend you. Continue to network, reach out to other businesses, and use word of mouth to keep your business afloat the first year.

Remember that turning a profit may not happen in the first year. It's most likely you won't see any money in the first six months. Be prepared for this, and expect it. Use caution in celebrating the first paid invoice, too. Put it back into the business instead of using it for a large celebration. Reward yourself, but remember that you want your business to last. Pay salaries, then divide up the money into services for your business.

THE FIRST CONTRACT

Getting the first contract comes from lead generation, which means finding the customers who need your services. Getting leads depends on what type of work, product, or service you offer, but there are some universal formulas to start. First, talk to your immediate circle and find out who knows who. Talk to as many people as possible, letting them know about your company, and ask if they know anyone who might need your help. Ask your friends and family to refer you to anyone they meet who needs your services. Remember that, while we all want to land the biggest contracts, it won't happen, especially during the first five years.

It is unrealistic to think that your first contract will be a big contract. Chances are that your contracts will be small until you build a track record. Be realistic and search for customers who are most likely to hire you. You can try to land a large project, and if you're lucky it will happen, but accept the reality that those big projects may have to wait until you have more reputation in your industry.

Finding leads on your own is difficult. It is difficult because so many businesses rely on lead generation companies. These businesses are set up to bring customers to you. They operate by project, hourly, or on a contract basis. Talk to your network and see who can refer a great service provider for your lead generation needs. You may be able to do it with a low budget, or you could spend a lot, so be realistic about both your needs and your finances. Pursue what you believe is the best option based on your budget and abilities.

In the beginning, the biggest setbacks for Sergio and his team revolved around getting the first few contracts. Generating leads wasn't a problem until people asked how long he'd been in the business. As soon as potential customers heard, 'less than a year,' they'd lose interest. It was a long time before he received his first contract. It took him six months to get that first contract for less than $8000. It was with a large company, and it took him another two months of negotiation before they finally issued the PO (purchase order).

ADVERTISING

As a small business, advertising will be different. In fact, one of your main selling points will be that by using a smaller company, the person working on the account will likely be more experienced, rather than a person working at a larger company, who would be assigned at a fraction of the cost. Typically, a person who decides to start his or her own company has a strong background and accomplishments, whereas larger companies may not assign an expert to the task. Your second big selling point is your availability, and your drive to keep the customer happy. Smaller businesses try harder because they have more to lose. How often can you call the CEO of a large corporation at home or on their cell phone if you have an issue? With smaller companies, all hands on deck mean the CEO is almost always available. Issues are handled faster, and with fewer people to go through. What I mean is that small companies are somewhat of a competitor for large companies because their customer service is better than large companies which is crucial information for large companies.

Sergio recalls taking calls at 3 AM or hopping in a plane last minute to the other side of the world simply because it was important for him to be there. He slept in a Japanese office for nearly a week when the earthquake of 2011 created some horrendous issues for his most important customer. He did it because he knew it was important to the customer, but also, by default, he was supporting the people who needed him. He helped the people recover their Telecomm infrastructure during the worst earthquake in recorded history. Few CEOs of large companies would do this for one of their customers. This is the type of customer service a large corporation simply cannot offer; this is your advantage.

You'll also need an elevator pitch and presentation decks. These are fairly customized to your company. The elevator pitch is how you sell your company in thirty seconds or less, and presentation decks are how you sell your company in a longer time frame, such as in a board room in front of company executives.

It is recommended that you spend some money in consulting to prepare these items. You can find these consultants, as well as other types of business consultants, through online platforms such as Fiverr, Upwork, Foundry, or by Googling "marketing consultants online."

RECEIVING PAYMENT

Moreover, when you're new in business, you won't get paid anytime soon. The company he received his first contract from had a 2-month payment policy, which in reality meant 90 days after the completion of the project. Even with a contract, large companies may delay payment. Unless you have the time and money to pursue companies legally, you'll typically wait for the payment. This delay meant Sergio received that first payment 9 months after the launch. His wife wasn't happy with the earnings after that long struggle, but this is the reality of starting a business in Silicon Valley. This is why you must be prepared to have little to no income during the first year of business, and why many startup business owners have a job on the side. It gets easier after payments and projects begin to overlap each other, but waiting for that first payment is tough.

PAST CUSTOMERS

One major problem for new businesses is that they lack a well-known past customer list, as was the case with Sergio's startup. When you approach a new customer, you talk about your previous clients and how satisfied they've been with your service. Without possessing an impressive past customer list, it can be extremely difficult to accomplish a breakthrough with larger firms.

In fact, when you somehow manage to win a contract from a large firm, as Sergio did for his business, it might forbid you from disclosing its name anywhere by NDA's (Non-Disclosure Agreement). In the periods following the first year, Sergio worked with a few large firms that everyone knows about. His business was located a few blocks from Corporate 50, a few miles from the largest high tech companies, and close to all these tech-giants, but they'd agree to work on the condition that we don't disclose this to the world. In other words, he couldn't add those big names to his list of past clients or his business profile. Sergio found ways around this issue, but all startups must be aware that it is a common problem throughout Silicon Valley.

Silicon Valley has a culture of secrecy that is born from protecting IP, which is why Sergio's business had to keep their portfolio quiet. This secrecy spills over into how vendors are treated. In some cases, it makes sense to hide who is working on a secret project or specific technology, but the fact is that, for the majority of vendors, there is no proprietary or strategic advantage to disclose that vendor X is working with a large company. However, large companies set the rules, regardless of the fairness of them. This means that secrecy is the norm across the valley. Unfortunately, small businesses simply have to deal with it.

Luckily, there is more than one way to handle secrecy. Ask smaller companies, in writing, if you can use their names in your portfolio. Use as many of them as you can, no matter their size. Even if they are so small that no one knows them, they prove your work track record.

Approach mid-size customers, especially if they are well known in the industry, and ask them to issue a press release with your name included. It can be as simple as, "we have signed a contract with..." or "company X has engaged with us..." There is no need to provide specific project details other than disclosing the relationship between your company and theirs. It helps you, but it also helps their overall corporate image. The press is good, and the fact that your company is Latino-led helps improve its image as a diverse company.

If your customers are the large corporations who don't let you use their name, refer to them as "one of the largest in the industry" or "one of the top 3 companies in the industry." This lets people know you are dealing, or have dealt, with some of the big guys in the valley, but you don't use their name. However, never lie about working with anyone.

The valley is smaller than you might think. If you lie and say you've worked with some of the top companies, the top executives who work for the company you're trying to work with will ask around. They'll find out if anyone has heard of you, and your lie will be quickly uncovered. You'll develop a bad reputation from which you may never recover. It's not worth the loss of everything you've worked toward to lie about the experience.

While it is difficult to change the non-disclosure policies for the largest corporations, you will be a lot more successful in landing a contract when the large companies want to show off their diversity. Checking the company diversity policies is a good idea before approaching any company.

COMPANY POLICIES

Company policies are typically published on their websites. They are also available by joining and attending MBE Certification organizations such as the Western Regional Minority Supplier Development Council. The fact that companies have diversity policies means that Silicon Valley is trying to work with more minority groups. It is still important to remember, however, that you will still be competing with dozens of other companies. Researching the diversity policy to make sure the company is worth the effort is using your time wisely.

Remember, too, that some of the largest companies in Silicon Valley, even though they have a public policy dealing with small or diverse suppliers, don't have a formal process to implement it as they don't want to "limit the freedom and creativity of their employees." This means that if anybody in the corporation can contract and purchase services then a formalized process to help diverse vendors may not work, as they are not a valid vendor; meaning, they do business with the vendors they have always been using. If that company has a diversity program and the diversity supplier management person can help, you may be able to get in the door, but the fact is that most large companies do business with other large companies, which is why you should look for smaller customers first. If a company is not open about its diversity policy, it might be better to skip them until you have more years of experience. Follow the path of least resistance, especially in the beginning. If you are pursuing a large customer and don't know anyone in the company who can help navigate the system, assign that company a lower degree of success. Move on and spend your energy on a company or deal that has a higher chance of success. For example, if you try to hunt for an elephant, you must also shoot rabbits so you can eat while looking for the elephant. Some new entrepreneurs get blinded by those larger deals and have little chance of success. It takes a long time for a large company to bring on a new vendor, especially one that has few years of experience.

Sergio has spent up to seven months on one agreement with larger companies, as everything must be reviewed by their legal departments. Every modification to a contract must be approved, and approval takes a long time. He has learned that weighing the degree of success is essential, and sometimes it's better to skip the lower degree elephants in exchange for rabbits that will feed you right now.

Although small businesses offer less expensive and more flexible solutions than large corporations, there are other, more complicated barriers in the way.

Some companies value diversity and allocate a billion dollars for doing business with organizations owned by minorities such as veterans, women, etc, but they belong to the Billion Club. Considering the vast number of startups in Silicon Valley, the chances of even making it on their targeted list are minute. Remember this roadblock as you approach large companies as a vendor. However, there is a way to try to get on their radar.

The best way to get into the Billion Dollar Club is to go through the MBE Certification Organizations which have Billion Club Member corporations as members and supporters of the minority companies. Basically, you have access to all these players in one place. You do have to apply for the MBE Certification and attend meetings, but these are rich target environments of corporations looking and competing to help minority own businesses.

On the other hand, some high-tech giants don't have any diversity programs. Instead, they believe in empowering their employees so that they can grow. They delegate tasks and allow employees to make key decisions so that their creativity is not hampered. These empowered employees may have the power to hire vendors and may be interested in diversifying their workforce. Look for a recent MBA within the company.

The recent MBAs who get hired by large companies are determined to prove themselves. As inexperienced individuals, they don't know how their firm can benefit from working with smaller players, nor do they have any idea about small firms that are proving their mark in the industry. As a result, they'd opt for the best names in the industry, giving entrepreneurs no chance whatsoever. Who gets fired for hiring IBM? But if they work with a smaller company and things didn't work out, their career could be at stake. This is when you need to prove your company's worth through quality work, positive word of mouth, and networking to meet these people. This is also why you need to calculate your chance of being hired and work with smaller companies until your reputation proceeds you in front of these individuals.

In reality, the real chances of catching a deal do not only rest on your strengths, weaknesses, and competitors but also on the mindset and culture of the company you're dealing with. There's nothing you can do that will get you a contract from such clients. Chasing them consumes a lot of time and there's little chance if not zero of working with companies like these.

Sergio soon realized that before negotiating with companies, it was important to research them and see whether they normally work with small players or not. He started examining companies' diversity policies for suppliers and whether they have clearly spelled out rules for the supplier selection process. This saved him a lot of time and made sure that he didn't chase a goose.

Look for diversity policies on company websites, or search for them through your Western Regional Minority Supplier Development Council. Make sure the company you're targeting works with small players, and if they don't, network more and build a larger portfolio of great work, awards, and happy customers.

RAPID EXPANSION

Sergio and his team experienced growth through the awards they won from their work. The team couldn't talk about their past clients, but they could show off their awards to new customers. This helped them grow their portfolio. Sergio knows that some of his customers would not have talked to him if he had not had these accolades. It's important to remember that someone deciding to hire or contract to smaller companies wants to make sure that he or she will not get fired for hiring the wrong company. The awards, combined with great references by word of mouth, helped mitigate that concern. If you do not have awards, rely on word of mouth and referrals to help gain new customers.

Interestingly, Sergio once asked a purchasing agent why his company did not get the contract when they had presented a better proposal at a better price point. He found out it was because he had gone up against IBM, and the purchasing agent chose the reputable company over the small business. That agent was forward in saying that he could not afford to make a mistake or have any issues, so paying double or getting fewer services wasn't his concern. Having awards, building great word of mouth from customer to customer, and gathering shining recommendations is crucial for smaller players to make it in a competitive market with an overwhelming amount of NDA's.

Among all the free advertising found in awards, word of mouth, and reputation, word of mouth typically works best for a wide range of small businesses. Gathering contacts through travel, networking, and doing a terrific job every time builds this type of advertising. When your first client is happy with your work, they will tell their business friends who might also hire you. Keeping word of mouth going is what keeps a business alive.

Other ways to network and keep word of mouth moving is through volunteer work with professional organizations. Sergio has and currently is, on many volunteer boards, where he is continuously socializing and building his community reputation. He has attended school events, seminars, social events, and more, where he has carefully networked over time. Meeting people, building trust, and convincing them to use your services takes time, so networking and word of mouth become the fruit of your labor. If you have a chance to meet someone and build a great relationship that will last a lifetime, you have a better chance of gaining a future customer. Sergio recommends spending 20% to 30% of your time developing networks with customers and the community to not only know how the market is behaving but to maintain these important relationships.

Entrepreneurs who switch career paths, however, will not have built a network. These individuals are starting from scratch, but will still succeed through networking, word of mouth, and attending conferences. There will be a steeper learning curve, but many people have succeeded this way. If you start later than everyone else, you'll either have to work harder to catch up or hire someone that has the experience to guide you, but it is still possible for you to succeed. You might also buy into a franchise, which offers training as part of their onboarding package. There are many different ways to catch up if you switch careers and it's best to know your business, but you can always get help catching up while you are building it.

During that first year, he did face issues in raising finance, getting contracts, receiving payments, facing the competition, etc, but things began to work out as he went ahead. Based on the contacts he developed earlier combined with a little bit of luck, he somehow managed to reach that 5-year mark.

There's a 70% chance of failure during the first year that keeps lowering as more years pass. Not a large number of firms survive beyond 5 years, so those that manage to reach that mark feel much better and confident.

Things got easier for Sergio's business after passing that monumental 5-year mark. He started receiving contracts from larger and well-known companies. However, as mentioned before, they didn't allow him to reveal this to others. Besides adding a high number of customers, he managed to win awards for his services. His sales cycle got shorter as more and more businesses began to trust him. The sales cycle improved from 1 year during the first year to 3 to 4 months after that magical 5-year mark.

If he didn't advertise those large company names in his company profile, then what led to this growth? Two major drivers caused this tremendous boost. Referrals or word-of-mouth worked. He made sure to deliver the best to every customer. This paid off; they went on to recommend his services to other players in the industry.

There also remained this magical number 5. In the first year, you're lucky to get a single contract. When you hit the 5-year interval, the question of "how long have you been in the business?" is no longer an issue. You get an edge over new firms. His customer portfolio began to expand rapidly, and the revenue started to surge at a skyrocketing rate. The largest customer, the well-known customers, still did not allow him to use their names on his website nor his sales presentations.

However, there are times when your fate betrays you when everything else seems perfect. He had an accident that turned everything upside down. He shares his experience with you to show you the pitfalls of owning your own business and how tenacity will carry you through it. You will still succeed despite pitfalls when you keep your determination.

Sergio (right) receiving the President's "E" award for incredible export services.

THE SKI ACCIDENT

He had a ski accident, in which all 3 tendons of his right leg were severed, which is a bigger deal in California as compared to other states. Since his right leg wouldn't allow him to manage the gas/brakes, he couldn't drive for at least 3 months. His business was inevitably impacted. He was out of the office for the next 7 months, during a busy time of the year. The most active months for deals and contracts in his industry were March through November. He was out of the picture from May to December.

No sales meetings were held for almost 10 months until February of the next year. Sometimes, you're tempted to think that you might have been better off as an ordinary employee. He was deprived of a paycheck for 10 months, but he continued to issue salaries to other employees despite earning no revenue. Likewise, medical insurance covers your medical bills when you're an employee. However, facing a severe injury as a business owner had its drawbacks.

A minor ski mistake led to a drastic downfall. The size of his company reduced in terms of revenue and human resources by almost 65%. No matter how much growth you're experiencing, small businesses remain vulnerable to problems until they are well-established. A small accident can force you out of business. Realizing how agonizing recklessness can be for him, his company, and employees, he said goodbye to skiing and has become very cautious and particular about the physical activities he performs.

THE STRUGGLE

His company did face the great recession of 2008–2009, but it didn't do any harm when so many small businesses were forced out of the industries. Surprisingly, he experienced skyrocketing growth during these two years until he was struck by a ski accident. That's when everything seemed to fall apart. Sergio won't forget how easy it would have been to give up and let the business fail. He remembers how hard it was to keep things going from a distance, and how close it all came to end. But again, truly passionate businessmen don't easily lose hope.

A large portion of the struggle was what he personally chose. A rational large business owner may have decided to lay off 40% of the employees, never thinking about issuing paychecks from their pockets. As a small business owner, Sergio was pretty close to all his employees. He never regarded them as numbers. He knew each one of them personally including their families, had lunch with the team, and had frequent interactions with them on and off work. It was more like a family. This is an advantage when things are going well, as the employees are generally more devoted to the company. During a personal tragedy, however, it is devastating.

As mentioned earlier, one of his biggest passions is to create jobs for people as there's nothing more rewarding for an entrepreneur than being a source of help and support for the community. Sergio would rather create jobs than make more money, let alone the idea of laying people off. One of the top-most drivers and motivations for him is the desire to help others, which inspires him to keep going when things are difficult. As a result, it wasn't just him who had the accident but the team and the company as a whole. This is another downside to owning a small business. If the CEO of a large business has to stay home for seven months, others run the business for him or her. As you can see, it's completely different in a small business.

In a setting like this, when you live, breathe, and see your employees as human beings, laying them off is not an option until you've tried every other approach. Since his company earned half of the revenue for almost a year, he kept on paying the employees out of his own reserves until both his business account and personal credit card account almost reached a zero balance. That's when he had no option but to lay off some staff. He decided to wait until the next year for layoffs for two reasons: He didn't want the employees to have stressful Thanksgiving and Christmas holidays because of losing a job, and finding a job between November and January is difficult due to the holidays.

BUSINESS RECOVERY & SUCCESS

The next few years following the ski accident were all about business recovery. Within a year, his company managed to rise back to where they stood before the accident. As they held on to their resilience, hard work, faith, and confidence in themselves, they began to grow even larger than before. Thanks to karma and the dedicated efforts of his team, after 15 years from the launch, Global4PL has managed to build up a sound reputation, serve high-profile customers, and win various awards for their accomplishments.

Their customers are their great assets, including the 800 lb gorillas. They highly appreciate all their customers, from small to large entities, each of which has helped them grow to what they are today. The company could indeed have grown faster with those big player names added to their profiles. Nevertheless, they have very high regard for the trust their customers place upon them, and they have succeeded through reputation. They are happy at what they do, which is to help their customers grow to a global level. They grow as their customers grow, and that's their business philosophy. As they view the valley, they see a land of upcoming opportunity, that still has room to grow in diversity and hiring of minorities.

CHAPTER FIVE

THE DIVERSITY CHALLENGE

Before moving on to the launch, Sergio had a good salary and great benefits as a director of a high-tech company.

It wasn't easy to walk away from a stable job. You have to be truly passionate about business ownership and have confidence in yourself. Most people would tell you to be prepared for six months without income but it can take significantly longer to break even depending on the nature of your business and the market dynamics. When it comes to serving high-tech customers in the B2B market, you can't expect a profit within a year.

LACK OF DIVERSITY: "UNCONSCIOUS BIAS" DISCRIMINATION

Remember the glass ceiling mentioned earlier? Sergio did face indirect to open discrimination. Although, according to his understanding, it was more about lack of diversity and cultural exposure than discrimination. With a lack of knowledge and exposure to other cultures, people tend to feel uncomfortable with those who are different.

What makes it worse is the tendency to develop generalizations and stereotypes about specific groups. This mental laziness doesn't allow them to personally interact and find out about a person who belongs to a minority. People are often conditioned into not favoring diversity and turn into open or accidental racists.

A HURTFUL EXPERIENCE WORTH MENTIONING

When you are starting a new business, you are not a household name yet. Your reputation is the only thing you have, so being professional even when you are being insulted is a must. You don't have to take the mistreatment but you must remain professional. There is nothing wrong with walking away or getting out of an abusive situation, but you must maintain a high level of professionalism. Always take the high road and never strike back at someone who pushes your buttons. Remember that when you confront a bad situation it is usually one person alone putting you in that bad spot. It is not all the people in that company. You need to recognize that it happens from time to time, deal with it, and maintain the professional reputation you've worked so hard to build. No matter how loudly the voices in your head are screaming "foul play," you must walk away respectfully. If you react, you will only reinforce the other person's negative view of you, no matter how unjustified the view.

Sergio and his team have been extremely lucky in their Silicon Valley interactions, as some of the relationships they have formed over the years have been with people that have been promoted and have opened other doors for the team. Sergio's team performed well for these individuals, making them memorable and bringing new customers in through these relationships. The key was in performance and professionalism. The team has continuously aimed to over-perform and be straight shooters, which has worked out well. If a customer is abrasive, they deal with it and continue to do the best possible job. However, Sergio has seen his share of the negative parts of being Latino in Silicon Valley.

Sergio understands this type of negative environment because he as well shares the lack of diversity and racist experiences. It wasn't even the earliest stage of his business. He had already spent years in the industry and had built a reputation as a professional in his field...There was a firm he'd been serving for several years. His company even won an award for extraordinary service to them. This company appointed a new director, and Sergio will never forget the first meeting he had with him or any subsequent meet-up. In fact, he remembers the first conversation, which went like this:

Director: "I am the new director and have heard a lot about you and your team. We're paying you a lot of money as well, but how do I know that you won't steal all our money and run away to Mexico?"

Sergio: (Speechless for 10 seconds): "Excuse me? What did you just say?"

Director: (Smirking): "I was just kidding."

Me: "Firstly, I am Chilean, and secondly, I have been in business for 15 years. To be honest, this is the first time someone has ever asked me that question. I have no idea how to answer because the US is my home. I have no plans to leave it, nor do I have a reason to leave."

Can you believe this? That was all at the first meeting. This is the type of situation you might also experience, so be prepared to always be professional.

A few weeks later on a Sunday afternoon, Sergio received a call from this person. The conversation went like this:

Director: "Sergio, I need you to do me a favor. There's this friend of mine who I've known for a long time and who's worked for me in the past. I need you to hire him."

Sergio: "I'm sorry, but we don't need another employee right now to fulfill your company's needs. Nor can I fire any of the existing team members to hire your friend."

Director: "Don't worry. I will revise the PO to increase so you can create a position in your team for my friend."

Sergio: "I'm sorry but I said that correctly: we don't need another member for our team to satisfy your company's needs. Plus, when meeting your CEO, I won't be able to justify the need to increase the PO to hire your friend."

Director: "Don't worry. I will deal with that."

Sergio: "By the way, who is your friend?"

Director: "Name X, worked for Company Y until recently."

Sergio: "I know him, he's a nice guy, but I won't hire him."

Director: "I know him and he's a good friend. I trust him and want him on our company's account."

Sergio: "Sorry again, why don't you open a requisition on your own and hire him directly for your company? I can't justify another person on your account. Even if you increase the PO, unnecessary hiring won't be financially feasible for my business."

Director: "Great. Have a great weekend."

Sergio: "You too."

During this conversation, Sergio was direct, polite, and knew enough about the industry to suggest an alternative solution. As expected, however, it wasn't over with this client. He received yet another call on a Sunday afternoon after a few weeks. This is what happened:

Director: (nicely): "Sergio, I need a favor from you."

Sergio (expecting the same previous demand): "Sure, go ahead."

Director: "I want you to travel with me to Las Vegas next week."

Sergio: "Las Vegas? What for? We don't have any project in Las Vegas; Las Vegas is not currently in our scope of work."

Director: "I need you to help me select your company replacement."

Sergio: "I'm sorry? Select my replacement?"

Director: "Yeah, I'm looking for a replacement I feel I can trust."

Sergio: "Do I even know the companies you're considering for replacement?"

Director: "Company A, B, and C."

Sergio: "They're all good; no question about that. Although they don't match our expertise and the services we provide, they're great companies indeed."

Director: "So I will let you know the dates for the meeting; either tomorrow or on Tuesday."

Sergio: "Sure thing. Let me know."

In this conversation, Sergio supported the decision of the director, stated why he thought the director should stay with Global4PL, but conceded when he knew the director's mind was made up. Sergio did go to Las Vegas to help the director interview all three companies for the transition. He remembers just looking at this director, noticing that he was friendly and relaxed when he was talking to a white male, but if the person that he was interviewing wasn't white, he just looked at them like they were going to mug him.

In the next couple of months, Sergio's team was booted out of the account. They let it go, knowing they had done their best work, and their departure from the corporation was no fault of their own. Every time he thinks of the episode, Sergio wonders how a person like that makes it to higher management without a trail of lawsuits, poisoning other organizations. However, he understands that his company reputation remains intact and positive because he did not react negatively to the treatment. This is the importance of staying professional in every situation.

Sergio truly believes that since he belonged to a minority, the company's management supported its director. Believe it or not, there's a tendency to believe in your own people, particularly those who look like you or talk like you. On top of that, there remains blindness to all the bias. Some corporations will look the other way when a director behaves this way for several reasons. Sometimes unknowingly, people have a lack of diversity in their views, thoughts, networks, and operations.

Sergio considers this an important event that altered his mindset about what to expect from people and organizations, and he passes this important lesson on to you. It will happen, so be prepared, and be professional. This experience made him accept the lack of diversity issues and mold himself and his business accordingly to avoid them.

He has come across as openly racist and a few ethically misguided people, but he never allowed anyone to harm him or his business. As he said before, it is better to walk away from a contract than work with a racist person or someone that will put you or your work down. He went to Las Vegas and helped the director interview replacements because he is a professional and he does not regret losing a big contract as he did not have to compromise himself to work with that director.

Sergio has developed a few rules of thumb when dealing with someone less than professional. He recommends the following in no particular order:

- Sleep well - As humans, we tend to react poorly when we're tired, so taking care of ourselves will eliminate any reason we may have to react poorly because we don't feel well.
- Do the right thing always - Doing the right thing always helps build a positive reputation, so do it, even if it is painful

or will cost you some business. Never forget that your reputation is not negotiable.

- Walk away - Walk away if the deal is no good, or if the situation is becoming overbearing. It's acceptable to excuse yourself to the restroom if you need to gather yourself, but always stay professional in front of the other person.
- Treat everyone as you would like to be treated - Even when that person in front of you is cutting you to the core, treat him or her as you would want to be treated.
- Never say or write anything in anger - Think before speaking, and ask someone else to look over written correspondence to ensure the tone is professional.
- Remember that the valley is smaller than you think - Someone knows someone who knows someone else. This is terrific for networking and terrible if you've developed a poor reputation. Your integrity, attitude, and composure are everything in the valley; don't throw it all away through one unreasonable act.

Remember that being professional doesn't cost you anything. It's better to go out of business than it is to lose your integrity because once you develop a bad reputation, you're finished in the valley. If you lose your business, you can always build again, especially on the back of positive integrity.

Sadly, you will encounter racism in your journey. It's important to understand how to handle it when it happens. First, consider the person inflicting the pain. If he or she is a lower-level employee, there may be ways to handle it within the chain of command. If the offender is at a high level, such as C-Level, then walking away may be the healthiest option. While there are times to fight back, there are also times to realize when the fight would jeopardize your integrity. You might not be able to win, and you might create more issues for yourself later.

If the person is at a low level and you decide to move forward with the matter, make sure to use the right avenues. The CEO is not always approachable for these issues, for example, due to chain of command and HR policies. If you approach HR and no action is taken, remember that HR's ultimate job is to protect the corporation. While these professionals want to create a great work environment for everyone, including vendors, sometimes they will ignore an issue, hoping it will go away. In this case, if you feel the corporation would still be interested in the incident, contact higher executives to make them aware of the situation. Always make contacting executives or CEO's the last step of the process, as CEOs tend to support their people and their companies first.

As you consider what to do about a bad situation, read the company to understand if moving through the chain of command is a wise decision. You've been working with the company, and you have a feel for their culture; you will be able to reasonably figure out if reporting racism is a good idea. You will be calculating your risk against fighting racism or discrimination, so make sure to think it through before acting.

Luckily, Silicon Valley is trying to follow the rest of the country in its rejection of intolerance, but some of the worst offenders remain at VP or C-Level positions. In these cases, there is a double standard where the rules are enforced for most but misconduct at a higher level is buried with settlements and NDAs. The fact is that the MeToo movement has helped open up talks about it but companies do not have to disclose when they have paid settlements or dealt with a repeat offender. This information is only released when it is reported as lawsuits in the media. Silicon Valley is on board against discrimination, but, like the rest of the country, it will take time to completely remove it.

WHY SILICON VALLEY LACKS DIVERSITY

Silicon Valley has attempted diversity on the surface. There are several different employees of different classes working across the valley. However, a closer look at individual corporations reveals a remaining lack of diversity in leadership roles and plenty of room for the valley to grow.

For example, if you look at a company that has a good percentage of employees of different classes but can't find diversity at C-Level or in the Board of Directors, the message sent by that company is that minorities are welcome as they help, but they are not allowed to hold leadership roles. This is the definition of racism at its core, and it is a hidden issue across the valley.

If lower-level employees are not able to access leadership, C-Level, or Board of Directors positions, that company is limiting their access to generational wealth and networks that produce wealth, which is where the valley stands currently.

The imbalance of races at the executive level and above is not because of racism but a strong tendency to stick to your circle of peers. The problem doesn't only originate in the corporate setting itself. It has its roots in elite colleges.

Students of Stanford and the University of California Berkeley develop a network of their own, and these universities are largely white. They will do business and hire people and startups around the same circle. They'll stick to people like them, those with similar backgrounds and experiences. While this isn't necessarily wrong, it certainly eliminates diversity from professional settings. It does not simply mean that a small group of college graduates discriminate against others, but it sows the seeds for a vicious cycle of pervasive lack of diversity throughout the region with a multiplier effect.

Besides the colleges, diversity issues also come from the top-most levels. Pick up any large company in Silicon Valley. Its board of directors will be males, whites and probably belong to a handful of elite US colleges. Consciously or unconsciously, most board members are programmed to believe that the associated responsibilities can only be handled by people like them, like the CEO of Wells Fargo who can't find qualify black managers due to his unconscious bias.

This idea automatically passes down the chain of command as minorities indirectly get the message that they aren't wanted by the companies for which they work. For any talented member from the minority community, the chances to rise to the top levels are close to zero. When you know you won't get promoted or even be recognized for your efforts, you don't want to stay in that company.

Currently, state laws require a certain number of females to be hired, but not Latinos, blacks, or other minorities.

The reason why the lack of diversity keeps expanding is that when people get too engrossed in their people, they become less and less able to see others, eventually becoming oblivious to the interests of other groups, especially minorities. To minorities, it's like watching others eating ice-cream from the outside window of an ice cream parlor. You can join their companies but because you're different, you're not welcome, not really, not deep down in their hearts.

Lack of diversity also created issues during the earliest phases of Sergio's startup. He has discussed how difficult it was to get that first contract. One of the most critical reasons behind the setback was the lack of diversity. Employees of high-end technology companies most often came from Stanford, Berkeley, and alike with 85% being white males, who would choose vendors who were either like them, white and male, or look for those within their college circle. Black or Latino rarely made it into these big companies, especially at that time. This is why Sergio developed a system of researching companies and approaching those with a diversified portfolio. It took more time than his competitors, but it paid off for him in the end.

The same problem would occur when approaching investors. They'd invest in look-alike and like-minded people and those they knew. Another criterion has recently been added: you need to be young. These people do value diversity, but their version or understanding of diversity is limited to all variations of white. This is why many Latinos use their funds for startup money; this is why it is so important to network and perform your tasks above and beyond expectations.

Hence, the policy to empower employees and decentralize the decision-making process leads to a lack of diversity and discrimination not only within their workforce but also extends to the supplier base.

Every challenge discussed above taught Sergio important lessons. As he moved forward and got past the initial stages of his business, he attained a peace of mind that made him just as comfortable getting out of a bad deal as agreeing to a good one. He realized that saying 'no' to a bad contract was just as beneficial and in some cases, even more important, than signing a good contract. Getting out of a place where he was not wanted was better than sticking around for a paycheck. This is why he started his own business where there was no glass ceiling.

LACK OF DIVERSITY: GENDER-BASED DISCRIMINATION

The corporate world is well aware of how rapidly the tech industry is taking over the world economy, with Silicon Valley recognized as the heart of innovative business ventures. Everyone seems to be impressed by the tech giants such as Google, Apple, Uber, PayPal,

Facebook, and Amazon, but few have looked into whether they even foster a progressive work environment.

You can't deny the fact that these companies have far more male employees than female employees. We can easily say that it has become an untold norm in Silicon Valley for companies to have male-dominated workplaces. The bad news is that the work culture in these organizations has been tailored to welcome male employees and to promote the "bro" mentality.

THE "BRO CULTURE," AND HOW IT IS AN ISSUE FOR STARTUPS

The "Bro Culture" happens when a company is working toward the wrong goals. Most founders of these types of companies are white males from a top university with wealth.

While there's no single definition for "bro culture," when you come across a company culture dominated by arrogant, obnoxious, over-confident white men, you immediately know what the term means. Success and winning are considered above respect in such cultures. Excess bullying and partying are common among the dominant employees and harassment is a norm. Excessive partying is often regarded as a motivation tool. You see managers screaming at their teams, while negative chatter and toxic gossip is the favorite pastime for employees. So how is the "bro culture" an issue for startups?

THE PACING ISSUE

One of the main issues with bro culture is that it values speedy growth, which is what makes them common in startups. Instead of realizing the benefits of organic growth, these startups are more concerned with achieving quick success. This is where things begin to go wrong. In the desire for quick success, they hire the wrong employees and seldom care about behavior. All they are concerned with is sales and they're often willing to compromise the ethical values for that. What else would be expected when they've invested millions into a tech project?

What they fail to account for is that brash behavior that accompanies soaring sales figures proves to be counter-productive. At times, the high seller is harassing another employee. When that harasser is a good performer, however, management refuses to take any actions despite knowing that there are behavioral issues. This pushes out good people who keep the company going in favor of those who aren't concerned with longevity, reputation, or anything else that keeps them in business. This also reduces diversity in the workforce.

When you keep on hiring the same group that keeps diversity away, you end up developing solutions that only cater to a limited group. On the other hand, a diverse team is more likely to come up with a flexible solution, leading to much higher profits.

INHIBIT PRODUCTIVITY

Since the "bro culture" is highly toxic, it costs enormous amounts of money to economies due to hampered productivity. In Silicon Valley, the culture develops gradually in startups and comes to a point when employee retention becomes a big challenge, which in turn slows down productivity and growth. The same was seen in Uber's case when teams were repeatedly changed and projects were constantly abandoned due to all the chaos. Employees become uncertain about the projects they are working on, and at times, they are overwhelmed with too many projects. In other words, the bro culture is a potential reason for failing startups.

The Need for Investment

Another reason why "bro culture" is a problem for startups is that they desperately need investment. Investors prefer to invest in ventures led by young white males who often do what you'd expect an immature guy to when he's given a lot of money. It's no wonder that a culture of excessive partying and reckless spending begins to surface. Bro culture is also a problem among investors. We'll talk about this later in the book.

STARTUPS WITH BRO CULTURE DON'T VALUE WORKPLACE DIVERSITY

Another reason why bro culture prevails among startups is that they don't prioritize diversity from the very beginning. Despite the productivity issues and toxic environment, the bro culture tends to flourish, for a short time. They ignore the benefits associated with workplace diversity and choose to stick to the bro culture. Again, this leads to catering to a narrow, specific group of people.

NO EFFECTIVE HR IN BRO CULTURE STARTUPS

Startups normally emerge from a single owner or a partnership, who don't consider hiring until they're overloaded with work. No effective HR exists at this point so ethnic and gender bias penetrates the hiring practices. Again, the young white males hire more young white males, who party together and push for higher profits above all else. The party atmosphere becomes a pattern of "bros hiring bros." If the teams keep on expanding without an HR, bad seeds grow, paving the way for a toxic environment.

THE "BRO CULTURE" IN SILICON VALLEY'S INVESTMENT FIRMS

A female entrepreneur raised her voice against a Silicon Valley investor in 2017, and about the bro culture environment. Another woman also revealed the increasingly suggestive messages she received from a venture capitalist. Also, a female CEO talked about facing sexist comments from an investor while raising funds for her online community website.

According to the New York Times, when these women reported the comments to the concerned investment companies or the investors' colleagues, they were ignored and threatened.

The experience shared by these women finally broke the silence as more and more female whistleblowers are coming out with their stories. Dozens of women working in tech startups have disclosed sexual harassment experiences with The Times. Most of these women back their claims with corroborating emails and messages from high-profile venture capitalists such as Dave McClure and Chris Sacca.

Silicon Valley must realize that it doesn't have room for the bro culture. Movements such as MeToo help expose it, but it remains an issue. Keep your company professional, be patient with sales and contracts, and aim for longevity over quick profits to help eliminate this type of toxic environment. Remember that running a business is a marathon, not a race.

MORE DISCRIMINATORY FACTS IN SILICON VALLEY

Even the few prominent women who made their mark in the tech industry aren't given due recognition. Yahoo's CEO Marissa Mayer and YouTube's CEO Susan Wojcicki may be the exceptions, but most female success stories are mostly associated with luck rather than diligence and hard work. In contrast, every time a man accomplishes something big, their accomplishment is always linked to ability and intellect. Women's work quality is doubted and put under scrutiny more often than that of their male counterparts. One fact that proves that women are considered less skillful than men is that their coding is double-checked more frequently for no apparent reason.

Github has proven this fact. It is a coding community that hides the coder's gender, helping reduce scrutiny against women. A study conducted on it revealed that when the gender was kept hidden, women's coding was approved more often than men's coding. Also, approach one female entrepreneur in Silicon Valley and ask them about raising finance. They'll tell you that venture capitalists prefer to back male-led ventures rather than female-led startups.

According to a 2016 Fortune Magazine report, male-led startups raised as high as $58 billion in investment, while those led by women only received $1.46 billion. While single men are favored over married leaders, the most underprivileged employee group is mothers.

Let's consider the idea of promoting a workplace that combines work, social life, and leisure. It provides haircuts, exercise sessions, beer-filled fridges, and meals to its employees so that they spend more and more of their time at work. The same can be said about Uber, which started offering dinner to employees at 8:30 pm. Adjusting to this culture means neglecting your family. This is where it hits the mothers, who are not likely to meet these unfair expectations. Companies simply don't care about parenthood, especially in the case of mothers.

Hiring someone who is organized and can multitask efficiently should be on any company's wishlist, yet companies overlook mothers, who develop these skills through caring for their children. Companies who do hire mothers understand their value, however, and know how to keep their loyalty while helping them stay devoted to their family.

Flexibility is key to support mothers, who we should all support, and value as we all have or had mothers whom we would like to see treated well. Businesses also need to remember that mothers largely care for the home and the children even when both parents are working full time. Women are often overwhelmed, especially when they are additionally forced to worry about keeping their jobs.

What's important for business owners to realize is that as long as the work is getting done properly, women can be afforded flexibility and other allowances to take care of their families. Women and minorities have lost most of the progress that has been made in the last ten years due to the pandemic and that is a generational problem that will need support from companies for years to come.

If women are going to bounce back, they will need more support, more flexibility, and more allowances from their employers.

Let's take the example of Janica Alvarez, the CEO of a breast pump company. Investors often ask her whether she can smoothly run the business while taking care of her children. This question never comes up for her husband, who is a business partner. Given the highly exclusive nature of the tech industry, it's getting increasingly difficult for women to break into the industry and progress based on merit.

QUESTIONABLE HIRING PRACTICES

While there's no conspiracy to keep women out of the tech game in Silicon Valley, the discriminatory hiring practices play a role to favor men over women. No matter how much you're told that Silicon Valley features a meritocracy-based industry, the reality is different. When faced with pressure to include diversity in their work cultures, the most they do is hire white females who would be a relative of the CEO or other founding member.

BENEFITS TO COMPANIES WHO PROMOTE WORKPLACE DIVERSITY

Now that it's clear that the lack of diversity is a significant problem in Silicon Valley, let's move on to why companies should consider resolving it. Why would Silicon Valley consider making changes to its culture when it's already producing successful companies every year? First of all, to improve on what matters the most to companies: the profits.

Emphasizing inclusivity in work cultures can increase company profits. Eliminating sexism has been shown to give a tremendous boost to customer bases. For example, the League of Legends is an online multiplayer game that used to be extremely tolerant toward toxic and abusive gamers, with a customer base of 67 million unique monthly users. Ever since the company started sanctioning abusive users with detailed explanations as to why they were suspended, the company experienced a huge surge in the number of unique monthly visitors that reached 100 million.

70% to 80% of all purchases are made by women, which is why it certainly makes sense to target gender. Yet, James Damore, a Google employee, pointed out that women are bad at computer programming because they tend to empathize rather than systemize. It's quite disappointing to see high-level professionals making such flawed statements. One of the biggest strengths of women is empathy, which proves extremely valuable to make businesses appeal to consumers. Since empathy helps companies obtain true insights into customers' needs and wants, it can be extremely useful for designing products and services that would click with the target audience.

The majority of diverse-leadership companies have reported huge profits, which is another reason why companies should implement workplace diversity. The IMF conducted a study with 2 million European companies. The results revealed that companies with women in 40–60% leadership roles experienced considerably higher financial returns. The research also tried to determine the underlying reasons for these findings, discovering that creativity and critical thinking are two critical characteristics in diverse workplaces that prove highly lucrative for the firms. Such firms benefit from the different approaches and perspectives of employees.

Also, because women are less inclined to take unnecessary risks than men (as a failure in a white male is perceived as a learning moment, while for women and people of color, failing can be career-ending), companies that have a relatively equal number of male and female employees are less likely to fail. The notion is backed by the famous tech investor, Roger McNamee, who states that gender-balanced firms are less likely to go out of business.

Hence, industry leaders should think about this. Associating talent with a single demographic is not sensible. If a group has been successful, you can't render other groups ineffective. Diversity should help companies become more financially stable and capable to achieve their goals. The tech companies, in particular, should put in a lot more effort to have a diverse workforce. This is a large reason why you should move forward with your business idea, and stay open to a diversified workforce as your company grows.

CHAPTER SIX

RECOMMENDATIONS FOR CORPORATIONS TO COUNTER DIVERSITY ISSUES

For this part of the book, Sergio would like to speak directly to corporations. Reading these recommendations will help corporations, but will also help startup business owners understand what pitfalls to avoid as their company grows.

Sergio has a Master's in Change Management and it does not take a master to tell you that looking at the problem of diversity is better suited for external consultants to help you deal with this issue. He can truly and honestly say that trying to solve a diversity & inclusion problem by yourself is almost impossible. Have you tried to smell yourself? This is similar to dealing with these issues. It is very difficult, but if you get someone else to look at the problem, you will know in one visit.

Sergio's first recommendation is to bring organizational development experts in to help you as your employees may not feel comfortable letting you know that the baby is ugly. Maybe they don't feel welcome or they have had plenty of unwelcoming situations which they have not complained about as they don't want to be singled out or suffer the consequences of speaking out.

Another reason is simple: If you have been in your organization for more than a few months, especially if you are the CEO or C-Level executive, you don't see culture anymore, you are part of it. Meaning, fish do not see the water. When an outsider comes in and looks at your company, he or she will see things clearly.

That is not to say that you need an HR consultant, in fact, you need an expert on change management that has experience in culture and changes in small and large groups. It takes a lot of experience to deal with this because C-Level is part of the problem. If your Board of Directors, executive team, and upper management are whiter than a glass of milk then you are part of the problem.

Sergio is also referencing the companies where the board of directors, executive team, and upper management are all white but they have a minority board member that serves in a lot of boards. You can tell someone is just checking the box.

Companies should look at their customer base make-up from a gender and racial point of view and ask themselves, do we represent our customer base?

Companies should aim to counter diversity issues from the very beginning because once the status quo is established, it becomes extremely difficult to change it. They can direct their HR departments to keep diversity in mind even before the company reaches 50 employees.

The key to resolving diversity issues lies in identifying the unconscious bias that exists within corporate cultures. If a company has a less diverse culture, it should take note of it and make a point to promote awareness about it. For instance, it's often the language companies use in their job listings that keep diverse candidates at bay. Once the unconscious bias is identified, companies should work proactively and purposefully against it. They should strive to promote a mindset of diversity and inclusion every day.

Talent is present in every community or group. Therefore, hiring professionals should target the most underrepresented groups. For instance, Pinterest asks for potential referrals from its employees for communities that are generally discriminated against.

The problem is that even the most diverse tech companies tend to choose homogenous profiles, especially when it comes to education. All hired candidates will have graduated in computer science from a prestigious university, for example. There is little chance for the candidate who had to work for their experience due to a poor income or other social disadvantages.

There has to be an end to this trend. Less traditional candidates coming from less prestigious colleges must also be given a chance. Instead of looking for a perfect resume on paper, companies should divert their hiring practices to onboarding people with the right attitude and capabilities, regardless of their academic profiles.

Inviting a diverse group of people from different academic backgrounds to the table enhances the workplace. By welcoming minorities to the decision-making tables, companies encourage them to seek out more opportunities. To embrace that, companies should foster a culture of respect, openness, acknowledgment, and inclusion.

There are many ways to promote inclusion. For instance, firms can encourage employees to bring cultural food so that others can try it. Likewise, holding small parties to celebrate their cultural festivals is another technique. These little gestures can do wonders to create diversity.

Tech firms can also promote inclusion by helping Latinos find leadership roles. All tech firms realize and are guilty of the fact that minorities such as Latinos are heavily underrepresented in these roles. This makes the Latinos less likely to step up when a promotion comes their way. To address that, companies need to have a concrete set of programs or policies for career progression. Managers need to become advocates for diverse employees taking initiative when opportunities arise. When minorities feel supported by their peers and supervisors and believe that they have the same skills, rights, and capabilities as their peers, that's a victory for the entire company.

Another way companies can promote diversity is by implementing workplace mentoring programs, which should not only engage management in diversity efforts but also encourage underrepresented groups to progress in the tech industry. These programs will provide a path to managers to develop assigned protégés, while diverse employees can use them to find themselves a mentor. The programs will then push the mentors to sponsor the protégés to hold assignments and training for diverse employees. The result of this will be an increased representation of minorities and women in leadership ranks.

Promoting diversity also has to do with humanizing our workplaces. This is particularly true in the case of women. They have the big challenge of being mothers, wives, homemakers, and employees. Companies have unrealistic expectations, especially from those in demanding positions. Creating diversity means their burdens need to be split. Reasonable work-life balance and family-friendly policies are what companies need to emphasize.

Investors are well aware of the fact that the executive members in most companies are white males from wealthy families. Since venture capitalists play a significant role in shaping the future of the corporate world, they must embrace diversity now and invest in diverse founders. There exist numerous businesses that are motivated to make positive changes to counter a lack of diversity. The investors must empower them. The positive change includes building cultures that foster inclusion, productivity, and equal opportunities for everyone. The growth of such inclusive cultures will create an innovative and more varied standard of business in the future.

But why should investors support tech startups that stress diversity? There are numerous benefits of this to the investment landscape and the wider economy. If you think about it, a startup investment landscape without diversity will only produce companies that can resolve issues of specific demographic groups. Given that 33% of the Unicorn founders came from the top 20 universities, each of which charges up to $70,000, it's quite clear which income group these founders came from. Not only are the founders similar to each other, but their thinking is also the same. It's no wonder that they tend to neglect to launch solutions that address the problems that don't touch their demographic.

On the other hand, diversity in the founding communities and open-mindedness from investors can certainly lead to newer ways of thinking and innovative solutions to solve problems.

Investors must also know that according to McKinsey, firms with the most diverse executive teams are 33% more likely to outperform others in terms of profitability. It's important to note here that companies founded by females typically have a more balanced composition of management teams and other employees than those founded by males. As revealed by FundersClub, companies with at least one woman founder employ 48% female employees, on average, compared to only 24% for startups founded by all-male founders.

Hence, investors should firstly hire diverse VCs and invest in startups with diverse founders.

Similarly, Angel investors should require a pre-defined level of diversity in teams before they commit any investments.

Consumers also have a role to play in addressing the lack of diversity. After all, companies are only there to address the problems of the consumers. While investors and business owners are likely to demonstrate bias, consumers, especially the millennial class, are determined to address the diversity issues. But that's not enough. Customers need to know what role they can play to counter the situation. The most obvious decision they can make is to buy from companies that have a good diversity record.

They can also promote the tech startups led by minority groups such as Latinos, Asians, women, etc. With so many social media platforms, this task is no longer difficult. Even if customers don't see any benefit, they should think of making the world a better place to live for everyone, where everyone has an equal chance for everything.

Currently, we are getting the results of what the system is designed to do. Unless there is a clear intention to change this outcome by broadening the founders/investors first 50 employees we will get the same results for the next 100 years and it may even get worse due to the latest changes in the economy and the type of company that is controlling the market. It takes energy to change the path we are in and it takes an acknowledgment that things need to change to make it more equitable to all colors, genders, and classes.

You, as a small business owner and consumer, are part of the puzzle. Keep these issues in mind as you grow your business and become larger. Become part of the solution to create a better Silicon Valley in the future.

CHAPTER SEVEN

THE LATINO COMMUNITY IN THE US

For Latinos and other minority groups looking for business opportunities in the US, Sergio will share insights about the latest trends and situations. To understand this, you need to consider the broader historical context of ethnic small businesses in the entire nation and the role institutions play within their communities. The business situation for Latinos also cannot be understood without a clear understanding of Latino demographics.

Generally speaking, the social and economic development of the Latino community largely depends on the community's capacity to enter the corporate world in enough numbers and posts, which in turn can improve their earning capacity. Yet, there are factors such as racial discrimination and lack of diversity that take things out of their control.

LATINO DEMOGRAPHICS

Demographics play a crucial role in shaping public policy in the US, particularly in urban cities. Marketing experts love demographics as it helps them know and understand the public and their needs. Without considering the demographics, it is next to impossible to obtain the entire picture of business ownership by people of color. To understand the qualitative importance of small businesses in the US, you need to know the relevant stats.

To present a better picture of the Latino enterprises, consider those quantitative and qualitative perspectives go hand in hand. According to the Pew Research Center, the Latino or Latino population in the US rose from 14.8 million in 1980 to 56.5 million in 2015. This dramatic growth is attributed to factors such as immigration, education, and other characteristics.

Latinos are the second-fastest-growing ethnic minority in the US after Asians. While the population is reaching new heights, the growth did slow down with the start of the 21st century for two major reasons: firstly, as a result of harsher immigration laws for foreigners in general, and secondly, due to the declining fertility rates among Latino women in the US.

Interestingly, the largest Latino population exists in the State of California. From 2000 to 2015, the Latino population in

California rose from 10.9 million to 15.2 million, representing a 39% increase. Throughout the US, the number of Latino births has been greatly outpacing the number of Latino deaths, reflecting the youthfulness of the Latino community. Those under 35 make up 70% of the total Latino market, representing a purchasing power of $300 billion. If the US society truly considers them a national resource, it will not only benefit the Latino community but also drive further economic growth for the country.

By 2060, the proportion of Latinos of the total US population is expected to rise by 28%. If that turns out to be true, every one in four residents in the US will be Latino.

INDUSTRY-WIDE CONTRIBUTION AND DEMOGRAPHICS

According to the Annual Survey of Entrepreneurs (ASE) 2016, most Latino-owned firms are comprised of younger management. Based on the North American Industrial Classification system (NAICS), heavy concentrations of Latino-owned firms are found in the Construction, Transportation, and Warehousing sectors, each of which is categorized under the "Non-manufacturing goods production & associated services" section. 26% of businesses in this category are owned by Latinos.

Latino-owned businesses are also dominant in the "administrative support, waste management, and remediation services" category, constituting 17% of the firms in the sector. Latinos even enjoy a promising share in the "leisure & hospitality" category. The community, however, remains significantly underrepresented in the "scientific, technical, and professional" category.

A major difference between a Latino-owned and non-Latino-owned business is the age of their respective businesses. 33% of the non-Latino-owned firms were started less than 6 years ago, while that percentage goes up to 50% for Latino-owned businesses. Of the total Latino-owned businesses, only 19% are at least 16 years old, as opposed to non-Latino-owned firms, 34% of which are at least 16 years old.

If we compare in terms of size, on average, Latino-owned firms tend to be slightly smaller than non-Latino-owned businesses. Latino-owned businesses are 50% less likely than non-Latino-owned businesses to have 100 or more employees, and even less likely to have 500 more employees. Considering the smallest of businesses, there is a considerably larger number of Latino-owned firms with 1 to 4 employees than non-Latino-owned firms with the same number of employees.

Latino entrepreneurs are typically younger than non-Latino business owners. Of the total number of Latino entrepreneurs, 33% are less than 45 years old, while the same metric for non-Latino entrepreneurs is 22%.

SIGNIFICANCE OF LATINO-OWNED FIRMS IN THE US

The economic importance of Latino-owned businesses is that the number of Latino entrepreneurs is rising at exponential rates and that one in four startups in the US is owned by a Latino entrepreneur.

The Latino contribution to new entrepreneurs increased from 10% to 24% from 1996 to 2016. The contribution of whites decreased from 77% to 56% during the same period. Hence, Latinos can play a crucial role in job creation.

Considering the consistent growth in the number and proportion of Latino-owned businesses, they have huge potential to benefit the national economy and the nearby communities.

LATINO SMALL BUSINESS TRENDS (BEFORE COVID-19)

The opportunities for startups and small businesses in the US have been improving over time. According to the "2017 Small Business Credit Survey" conducted by the Federal Reserve Bank, the majority of the small businesses experienced growth, 57% reported profitability, and 53% reported a rise in their revenue. Experts predict rapid economic growth in the upcoming decade, with 72% of the US firms expecting a further increase in their revenues and 48% expecting to recruit more staff in every subsequent year.

However, the climate of small businesses greatly varies in terms of gender, ethnicity, income, and race. From 2007 to 2012, the number of Latino-owned businesses increased by 47%. On the other hand, the number of non-Latino-owned businesses decreased by 2% over the same period. While Latino-owned businesses thrived well before, during, and after the 2008 recession, the business opportunities, challenges, and performances of these firms largely differed from non-Latino-owned firms, especially those owned by white males.

An important thing to know is that Latino entrepreneurs are more likely to launch their startups out of necessity than white and Asian entrepreneurs. This is commonly known as necessity entrepreneurship. By definition, it means that if you were unemployed before launching your business, you're pursuing necessity entrepreneurship. The unemployment rate for Latinos in the US in 2016 was 5.4%, which is higher than the 4.9% overall employment rate at the time.

As you read earlier, necessity entrepreneurship doesn't apply in Sergio's business case. He had stable, well-paid employment, which he left to launch his business. Thus, like most white and Asian entrepreneurs, he began his business out of opportunity and passion. This is referred to as opportunity entrepreneurship.

However, motivations are merely the reasons to start a business. They don't determine the outcomes or measure the success of the business. They require the same amount of determination and passion to succeed.

ACCESS TO FINANCE

When it comes to access to financial capital, a great deal of disparity still exists between Latino and non-Latino entrepreneurs. The Stanford Graduate School of Business's Latino Entrepreneurship Initiative (SLEI) found that 69% of Latino entrepreneurs rely on their savings to fund their startups, as opposed to 62% of white startups. 11% of non-Latinos access funding from commercial banks, as compared to only 6% of Latinos.

Besides, the wealth gap between Latinos and non-Latinos present further challenges in raising financial capital. With a median wealth of only $13,730, Latinos possess only 10% of the median wealth of white Americans. 12% of Latino businessmen obtain funding from their friends. The problem is that the financial capital available to people who largely rely on self-finance or friends' savings is considerably smaller than the pool available to those who are more likely to turn to financial institutions.

Kauffman Foundation states that startups with $5000 or less in financial capital have a 23% more chance of failure compared to those with a startup capital of $100,000, an amount that's more than 7 times the average of Latino wealth. Hence, funding is a huge challenge for Latino business owners in the US. This is why networking, borrowing from friends and family, working while building a business, and talking to mentors are so important to Latinos. You might start behind others financially, but, as Sergio's story proves, it doesn't mean you have to stay there. There are many ways to find financing for your business.

While it has been mentioned that finding investors is difficult, it is not impossible. There are several types of investors for several types of products and business types. Most important, though, is if your business has the new hot commodity or the latest and greatest technology. For example, it used to be the up-and-coming social media webpages that got investors, then it was delivery services such as Uber, now it's Artificial Intelligence. You can chase these investors, but remember that you have to have the shiniest new product or technology to get any attention. If your idea doesn't have a chance to be a Unicorn, approaching large investors will not be your best chance to get funded. You will hear that money is flowing, and the amounts are in the billions, but if you take an honest look at the types of companies getting funded, the list is narrow.

Don't lose hope yet. However, if you are small and don't have the newest shiny design, you might still find funding from Angel investors, who are private investors looking for greater returns that close to zero from banks and financial institutions. Google "Angel Investor's Network" to find a list of places offering connections to Angel investors.

ACCESS TO EDUCATION

Access to education presents further challenges to the Latino community. Only 13% of the Latinos in the US hold college degrees, compared to 50% of whites and 29% of Asians. Non-Latinos are thus more likely to have a college degree in the US. However, if we specifically talk about Latino entrepreneurs, they are two times more likely to hold a college degree than an average Latino in the US. Also, Latinos with college degrees are more likely to make revenues over $100,000 than those without a degree. Consider all options in schooling, from how to get a degree to one-time business courses you might take that would contribute to your goals.

BUSINESS GROWTH

One important measure of business performance used in previous studies is the proportion of firms generating at least $1,000,000 in annual revenues. It was previously mentioned that Latino-owned firms are generally smaller than those owned by non-Latinos. Only 21% of Latino-owned businesses earn revenues higher than $1,000,000, as opposed to 32% of white-owned firms. Additionally, the number of white-owned firms is much higher than Latino-owned firms. Moreover, Latino-owned firms are twice as likely as non-Latino-owned firms to fall under the category of micro-enterprises, or those with less than $100,000 in revenue.

Hence, in terms of growth, Latino-owned businesses lag as compared to other businesses.

FINANCIAL SETBACKS TO LATINO-OWNED BUSINESSES

Despite experiencing growth and positive performance outcomes, Latino-owned businesses, particularly startups, continue to face financial challenges. The Small Business Credit Survey conducted by the Federal Reserve Bank asked small business owners whether they faced any financial difficulties during the first 12 months of the launch. 71% of the Latino business owners reported financial difficulties compared to 62% of the white business owners. When asked about each specific challenge, Latino entrepreneurs reported higher difficulties for each of them compared to the white entrepreneurs.

One of the most common problems for small firms is paying the operating expenses. The same is regarded as the top financial challenge for Latino-owned businesses.

Another major financial setback is the credit availability issue. Based on the 2017 SBCS, 41% of Latino-owned businesses reported difficulties in credit availability compared to only 28% of white-owned businesses.

Even the Latino-owned firms that have been operating for quite a while and have grown to scale continue to face trouble paying operating expenses and obtaining credit. Over 44% of the established Latino-owned firms face these issues, which are hardly faced by established white-owned firms.

All these facts have significant implications for the growth of Latino businesses in the US. According to the 2017 SBCS survey, 61% of the Latino-owned firms had specifically applied for financing to expand their businesses. Credit availability issues to these firms will defer investment and hamper their growth.

REASONS FOR LIMITED ACCESS TO CREDIT

As discussed, Latino-owned businesses experience more financial shortfalls than white-owned businesses. Based on the 2017 SBCS findings, the most apparent reasons were their lower credit scores and limited credit experiences than the white-owned businesses. The reason why Latino-owned firms were less likely to cite a heavy debt burden was their limited access to credit in the first place.

Consistent with the pattern that a high proportion of Latino-owned businesses are startups and small firms, their credit risk was likely to be much higher than white-owned firms. 49% of the Latino-owned firms report carrying medium to high credit risk compared to 29% of the white-owned companies.

CHAPTER EIGHT

CORPORATE STANDING OF LATINOS IN SILICON VALLEY

According to the Latino Foundation of Silicon Valley (HFSV), Latinos represent a massive 30% of the active Silicon Valley population. Nevertheless, they remain a distinct minority in tech companies in Silicon Valley.

In terms of employment, they make up only 6% of the staff in tech firms compared to 22% of non-tech firms. High-tech companies such as Apple and Yahoo! openly express that their manpower is shy of Latino or black people, who never become more than 5% of their workforce. Asians, particularly Indians, on the other hand, have penetrated the tech industry with great success.

The numbers further narrow down when you find Latinos in the rank of investors and entrepreneurs. According to the Equal Employment Opportunity Commission, less than 1% of the tech firms were founded by Latino entrepreneurs.

As discussed in the 'lack of diversity section', the circle of investment and trust that stands as the heart of the tech industry doesn't appreciate multicultural values. Silicon Valley's limited circle of mentors and investors is often referred to as the "white boy's club." This shows the gravity of the situation in the region.

The tech industry in the Valley demands a high level of technical education or qualification, which most Latinos lack. No wonder the credit availability to Latino entrepreneurs remains a challenge in Silicon Valley.

However, the scenario is undergoing a dramatic change. Different organizations and programs have been initiated to provide investment, tools, and other necessary support to narrow down the opportunity gap for Latino entrepreneurs and help them follow the technological game of the Valley. When more young Latinos, such as yourself, build businesses in the tech industry, Silicon Valley will have to take notice. Things will begin to change and future Latino startups will have an easier path to success.

CHAPTER NINE

INITIATIVES TAKEN TO ASSIST LATINO STARTUPS

If you see yourself a Latino Silicon Valley tech entrepreneur in the future, here is a piece of good news for you: several organizations have come into being to support prospective Latino startups. Here are the most common initiatives.

MANOS ACCELERATOR

Having experienced the unavoidable reality of the big, unwelcoming financial circles of Silicon Valley, successful Latino entrepreneurs, Edward Avila, David Lopez, and Sylvia Flores collaboratively launched the Manos Accelerator. Edward Avila was concerned about the loneliness of Latino entrepreneurs in the entire US.

Launched in 2013, it works as a business incubator supported by Google to develop a network of Latino investing angels to provide financial support and mentorship to Latino entrepreneurs hoping to make a mark in the ultra-competitive landscape of Silicon Valley.

If you haven't studied at Stanford or Berkeley, that's no longer a problem. With the creation of influence networks through the Manos Accelerator, your ethnicity is no longer a weakness. After all, you have access to the resources and mentorship backed by Google. To date, the organization has given birth to and nurtured several Latino startups such as Audive and CoupleCare. It continues to work on some others.

One startup associated with the Manos Accelerator, Dream Tuner, was founded by Alejandro Carrasco. The venture was a web platform designed for independent musicians looking to get in touch with musical discoverers. According to Alejandro, all the information on how to organize and launch the startup was available online, but he and his team needed solid mentorship. The participation provided him that mentorship to make changes and polish the idea.

However, he also pointed out that accelerators are only helpful if they're properly organized, connect you with the relevant experts, and genuinely teach you something.

Find Manos Accelerator here: https://manosaccelerator.com.

HISPANIC FOUNDATION OF SILICON VALLEY

This foundation doesn't directly support Latino-owned startups but endorses the overall welfare of Latino professionals in Silicon Valley. It aims to boost and promote a better standard of living for Latinos living in the region in terms of education, professional opportunities, leadership, recognition, personal achievements, etc.

The foundation members believe that the major cause of Latino underrepresentation in the high-tech business environment of Silicon Valley is the low numbers of Latino graduates in technology, engineering, and mathematics programs. As a result, they've joined hands with ALearn and Silicon Valley Education Foundation to improve the future job prospects for Latino individuals. Their algebra and mathematics programs are examples of this.

Sergio has been a proud member of the board for the Latino Foundation of Silicon Valley for over 8 years and could not be more proud of the work they do for the Latino community in Silicon Valley.

Find Hispanic Foundation of Silicon Valley here: www.hfsv.org.

SILICON VALLEY LATINO LEADERSHIP SUMMIT (SVLLS)

Introduced by Frank Carabajal, SVLLS is an event held annually to inspire and share actionable guidelines for future Latin American leaders to be successful in Silicon Valley. Every year, it attracts a huge Latin American audience that's interested in education, business, industry, enterprises, government, etc.

If you see yourself as a potential Silicon Valley entrepreneur, you simply can't miss this event. Renowned corporate personalities and MBAs attend and talk about everything you need to know about success. There's no better event than this to expand your business network, which is the key to entrepreneurial success in Silicon Valley. Part of this event includes the Young Latina Project (YLP), which encourages the participation of Latin American women in the fields of engineering and technology in Silicon Valley.

Find Silicon Valley Latino Leadership Summit here: https://svlatino.com.

STANFORD LATINO ENTREPRENEURSHIP INITIATIVE

Remember the aforementioned credit access issues for established and scaled Latino businesses? This is where the Stanford Latino Entrepreneurship Initiative helps. This is an initiative launched by Tiq Chapa to provide a digital course with resources and access to capital to Latino-owned businesses having at least $1 million in income.

The entity also aims to promote positivity in terms of the Latin American representation situation in Silicon Valley businesses. While it recognizes the low presence of Latinos in the Silicon Valley business world, it emphasizes that the numbers are going up. Based on its findings, more than 1000 Latinos are employed at 10 tech giants in Silicon Valley. It also states that 65,000 Latinos graduate from US colleges every year in programming and software development.

Besides sharing such positive insights, the organization believes that given the current 4 million Latino entrepreneurs in the US, there is a high probability that Latin American professionals will launch businesses in the future. Thus, the program seeks to give them a positive turn.

CSIT-IN-3

This is a 3-year graded program in Computer Science and Information Technology that replaces the traditional 4-year Bachelor programs. While it is not specifically targeted to Latin Americans, over 90% of the attendees are Latinos. One of the founders of this program, Joe Welch, states that this program aims to diversify the manpower in Silicon Valley by eliminating the pervasive lack of diversity. One of the most amazing aspects of this program is that it provides internship opportunities at the top tech companies of Silicon Valley to qualifying students.

Hence, Silicon Valley is indeed a difficult place to start, but if you're a determined Latino, you can find your way into the tech game. The underlying fact is that you have much more support than in the past. Don't hesitate to reach out to the initiatives mentioned above. There's also a podcast named El Valle de Los Tercos available. It shares amazing insights into Latino life in Silicon Valley. Also, start attending the Silicon Valley Latino Leadership Summit from now on to develop your business network and obtain important industry insights.

Find CSIT in 3 here: www.csin3.com.

Find out more general information about the Latino business community here: LBAN/Latino Business Action Network. www.lban.us.

CHAPTER TEN

A FEW THINGS THAT WILL HELP YOU BE SUCCESSFUL

Certain characteristics and traits make people more suited to successfully launching and nurturing a business venture than others. Some of them are innate, others are learned with real-life experiences and struggle. It makes sense to include the most critical ones in this book. Prospective Latino entrepreneurs, and every other individual aspiring to be a successful businessman, should consider developing the right attitudes and characteristics from the very beginning. This will serve you as your business grows and will help inspire much-needed diversity throughout Silicon Valley.

Keep in mind that not all entrepreneurs, especially those of today, succeed merely out of luck. You may have heard about backstories of successful entrepreneurs who once only managed a lemonade stand or ran a newspaper delivery route. Things are different today. Today, most businessmen succeed or fail based on their personality and experience. Based on Sergio's experience and the insights he obtained, the following actions play a vital role in entrepreneurial success.

SPEND TIME NETWORKING

Entrepreneurship is often perceived as a one-man show, but entrepreneurial success largely depends on possessing a network of like-minded people who you can interact with and who can support you when needed. It proves extremely valuable to be surrounded by people who are good problem solvers.

Sergio has seen for himself that great ideas often come from productive conversations and brainstorming sessions. It's not that a person suddenly comes up with a world-changing idea, translates it into reality, and starts earning millions. Developing a large the professional network provides multiple opportunities to brainstorm and evaluate your concepts and ideas with other people as well as obtain new insights from them.

Networking doesn't just help with idea generation and execution. As you see the benefits, you will want to socialize with more and more professionals to nurture your business and take advantage of newer opportunities to adapt to the changing world. With a large professional network, your business should grow at a faster rate. Introverts rarely make it to the top. During difficult times such as a recession, even business survival becomes a huge challenge.

Hence, wherever you are now, start socializing with talented and educated people around you. If you're a student, surround yourself with creative people who like to do something new and aren't afraid of embracing change. The same is recommended if you're an employee who is working on a side hustle which you want to grow into a large firm.

Try to network face to face, if possible. We are all humans, and we need personal contact to get to know each other better. A good part of communication is unspoken, so over-the-phone networking isn't as ideal as in-person conversations. Pick up the game of golf, if you have a chance, as a significant number of businesspeople enjoy the game. Playing around gives you a unique opportunity to talk to another person for several hours, helping to establish a personal relationship.

Finally, when approaching a CEO or possible investor, remember that businessmen are human beings, just like you. They are often placed on a pedestal, but they share the same basic human needs. Approach them just like any other person while staying professional. Keep in mind that they are often busy, and are used to people trying to sell them something right away, so you may need to take some time for them to let their guard down. However, this is all part of networking, but you are still networking with human beings. Be professional, be yourself, don't oversell, and have a human conversation.

PAYING ATTENTION TO WHAT PEOPLE NEED

As simple as it sounds, entrepreneurship is about solving problems for ordinary people. A good entrepreneur will have a clear idea about the psyche of people and about the basic necessities of a happy life. The most basic needs include food, shelter, entertainment, companionship, and simplicity. People have a strong desire to obtain these things. By knowing these aspects and what people desire, you're able to spot opportunities to help them in their pursuit of those needs and improve their experiences.

Ideas that genuinely help people get essential things in life become popular immediately. People will engage with such ideas and come to rely on them. A clear example is the renowned social media platform, Facebook. Mark Zuckerberg realized people's need to socialize with others and stay connected. It's no wonder that people quickly embraced it, and today, it's the most popular social media platform that people rely on to stay connected with their friends and loved ones.

Hence, to be a successful entrepreneur, you will need to learn to gain perspective about the inefficiencies and problems around you and relate them to human needs. You never know when you will be able to discover a significant market gap that will generate tons of money for you.

BE PROACTIVE

However, to be able to identify inefficiencies and capitalize on them, you need to be proactive. Once you've discovered an inefficient situation, being proactive proves beneficial in devising a solution or product for it. Part of the reason why Sergio started Global4PL was to address the difficulties he saw in expanding beyond international boundaries. These problems were associated with freight forwarding, customs brokerage, compliance, and the lack of technology to automate the related functions. He personally faced these challenges with his previous business venture.

He was impatient and instead of waiting for someone else, he started thinking of ways to solve these problems on his own. Thanks to his need to act, he finally developed a high-sought solution that makes things remarkably easy for businesses that operate globally.

Generally, people face problems every day and they do realize that there's a better way of doing things. If they are provided with that better way, they'll take it. What's different about entrepreneurs is that their impatience motivates them to take action and devise a solution for everyone.

CURIOSITY

Another important trait is curiosity about the different ways in which technology advances around the globe. If not for this trait, Sergio wouldn't have been able to succeed as a businessman.

Each country has its own cultures, social climates, business dynamics, buying behaviors, needs, and preferences; hence, each economy is unique. Likewise, people in diverse countries have different problems. To resolve them, a handful of talented individuals come up with solutions that change the lifestyles of people. All this depends on the availability of technology.

Since it proved insightful, Sergio always encourages aspiring students to pay a visit to China to personally witness how technology is developing there. Given the problems he observed around him, Sergio was curious to discover ways to resolve them through technology. While he didn't find the answer in China, he learned a lot of other things there and developed his professional network. If you're a founder or want to become a founder, don't lose any opportunity to travel to business hubs. They should offer you valuable experiences. Plus, regardless of whether you travel or not, keep absorbing ideas and concepts from your experiences. Stay curious about the world to keep a sense of cultural knowledge that will contribute to how you run your business.

Keeping curiosity open will keep you open to different solutions, and when one way doesn't work, reach for another way. Always ask, "what if," and always try to find the answer. Make sure to keep an open mind to every answer, staying flexible to all solutions.

BE FLEXIBLE

Entrepreneurship is not rocket science, but it's not that easy either. Successful entrepreneurs are those that are able to find the right combination of stubbornness and flexibility. Stubbornness is the need to be persistent in pursuing your business idea and keep working on it despite criticism from others and your own doubtful thoughts. You must also be flexible enough to recognize the mistakes you made on your first attempt. You may have launched a product, but later on, you may find out that you failed to target the right people or it would be more successful in a different location or market. Understanding the problem is the first step toward finding a solution. If you fail to realize such important facts, others may eventually use the same idea and do things right, eventually overtaking you in no time. It's important to respond to market dynamics and customer demands and tweaking your idea to accommodate them.

Even if you can't find an immediate solution to the problem, be prepared to accept what you're doing wrong and be flexible to recognize solutions too. Reach out to others for help, if necessary, and read everything you can find on solving the problem. Remember that one person alone can't always see every possible solution. Flexibility is a critical entrepreneurial characteristic and one that will help you in your most stressful moments.

BE PASSIONATE ABOUT YOUR BUSINESS

Have you ever wondered why some people are ready to give sweat, tears, and blood to achieve certain goals? It's their passion that motivates them. You may have multiple passions, but what's that major aspiration? Working toward multiple passions can also produce inefficiency. You need to focus on one passion so it is easy to justify the time and effort you put into a project. You might be pulled in different directions but with experience, you will be able to stay focused. When you work relentlessly to fulfill your passion, success will become inevitable.

TRUST YOURSELF—BELIEVE IN YOURSELF

To be an entrepreneur, there is a clear degree of confidence which you need to keep inflated. If you are not comfortable taking risks and don't have a healthy belief that you will make it, you won't. If you are afraid but you know that you will make it, you are an entrepreneur without faith. Faith, confidence, or that gut feeling that you know you will make it is a must. If you don't believe you won't make it, you won't make it. If you have that fear but know you will make it, find faith in yourself.

When an entrepreneur starts out, there aren't many people who believe in their idea. In fact, some people will keep pointing out negative aspects and try to discourage them. To stay persistent, entrepreneurs must possess self-belief, which helps them thrive in the beginning. They need to have confidence in themselves and in the ability to execute the business idea they came up with. You should not think you are always right, but as an entrepreneur, you should have that natural inclination toward staying steadfast and trusting personal capabilities, even when others don't.

Self-belief requires entrepreneurs to stay optimistic. During the earliest stages of a business, you need to view the positives and limit your thinking about the possibilities of failures. Such a mindset helps you remain tough and your business to thrive. However, this doesn't mean that you close their eyes to problems. Despite staying positive at all times, smart entrepreneurs remain conscious of the potential challenges and look for ways to address them.

NEVER STOP LEARNING

There are many ways to keep learning, from online classes at top universities, to free courses, to YouTube channels, to trade magazines, and more. You can take classes in your area of expertise or more general courses for other aspects of your business, such as a psychology course for people skills. It's nice to continue your education to keep your business knowledge up to date, but it's also a good idea to continue to learn about the rest of the world. General knowledge makes you well rounded, and makes it easier for you to have conversations while networking.

Learning exercises your brain, and without it, the brain becomes stagnant. Focusing on only your industry streamlines you into only interacting with others in your field while learning about a range of topics helps you branch out to other industries. You never know where you might find customers, so it's always wise to know how to talk to everyone you meet.

It's important that you position yourself as an expert in your field as you navigate through learning opportunities. Keep up with trade magazines, online pages, updates to the industry, and general business information to stay on top of everything that's happening. The world changes fast, and you don't want to be left behind.

Attend events for both education and networking opportunities. Join trade groups and volunteer whenever possible. Sergio has been a member of several trade groups and has even been President of some organizations. The education and network built here will be invaluable to your business. Remember, however, that conferences are not a place to sell. They are a place to learn and to meet others who might help you in the future.

Successful entrepreneurs never stop learning. They keep their boundaries open to valuable information, leadership, and management for as long as they live. Likewise, they're always looking to be more effective and efficient than before. They often want their companies to be better, faster, and more dynamic than any other organization around the globe, which is why their characteristics transfer into their teams as well. This way, they're able to adopt a situational management style, which means they'll adapt to any situation and people they're faced with. They develop a great intuition regarding what works under what conditions, which can be referred to as "selective flexibility." Depending on what they think is good for the company, they will be flexible when required.

BE DECISIVE—MAKE INFORMED DECISIONS

Being decisive has often been linked to risk-taking abilities. However, there is more to being decisive. What makes entrepreneurs incredible risk-takers is the ability to assess the risks and the associated outcomes in a way that others cannot. Hence, their decisiveness is a combination of risk assessment and risk-taking. If you think about it, risk assessment is more important as it helps predict the outcome of the risk, which makes the entrepreneurs make decisions. Since they're able to see over the horizon, they don't view risks the way others do.

They're much more tolerant and resistant to ambiguity and uncertainty, both of which will not prevent them from making decisions. In fact, the most talented entrepreneurs are determined to make decisions in a high-risk and uncertain environment because they want to break the competition apart. Anyone can demonstrate decisiveness in a low-risk and highly predictable environment.

More importantly, entrepreneurs have an entirely different attitude toward mistakes and failures. Being decisive doesn't necessarily mean that all their decisions will prove successful and produce the desired results. However, when they do make a mistake, they take responsibility and view it as an opportunity to learn and improve. Just as they're not afraid to face failures, they demonstrate a tough come-back, adjusting and correcting their course of direction to achieve their business goals.

BE COMPETITIVE

In a global economy, you have competitors everywhere. Don't sleep on your laurels and keep moving. Stay sharp. The real competition is not always apparent. Some fierce competitors won't explicitly declare competition against you. Their tactics remain hidden but in time, their market shares indicate that they're determined to win and more importantly, they don't like to lose. The most ambitious entrepreneurs don't just want to stay on top, they strive to leave their competitors in the dust.

Staying competitive is a combination of different sets of skills. The first set is technical expertise, which is being the best you can be at what you do. You also need to be a generalist who understands every area of your business, or someone who brings in people to compliment your weak areas. Again, learning is essential in staying above the competition. As soon as it seems you don't know what you're doing, the customer will go somewhere else.

As you build your business, you will learn your weaknesses. Any apparent weaknesses will be preyed upon by the competition, so they must be addressed immediately. If education does not help eliminate a shortcoming, hire someone whose strengths complement your weaknesses. There are several sites where you can locate experts affordably who will be able to work out your problem in a short amount of time.

Some business owners don't like consultants because they are expensive, but this is where you will have an edge on the competition. You know that the return on investment (ROI) for consulting services is huge. After you address and fix a problem, you can get back to work and serve the customers better than your competitors, because you found a weakness and repaired it. Put aside the ego and hire someone who will tell you honestly where your problems lie. A recommendation for change is not a statement that you've done something wrong; instead, it is an idea that will put you ahead of other businesses.

Luckily, startups have different avenues to stay ahead of the competition in Silicon Valley. As a small company, you are more nimble than a large company. You can fluctuate price when necessary, your line of communication is shorter, providing better customer satisfaction, and you have more up-to-date solutions, as your livelihood depends on you knowing your industry. Bigger companies simply cannot provide these types of services.

Specific advice for Latinos to stay competitive is to targe other Latino business owners in the short term for networking and referrals, then expand the network as soon as possible. Latinos have not been as proactive at helping each other as much as other groups, but we need to change this to get economies to scale.

Another option to stay competitive is to join CEO roundtables or groups where CEOs and business owners meet to discuss their problems and concerns. Normally, these are expensive and depend on what kind of product or service your company offers. However, there is no better way to get to know CEOs, their businesses, and how they are operating within the industry.

Use these opportunities to keep networking to keep your business at the top. Remember that people like to do business with those they know and trust, so network to make professional colleagues and friends who will lead to sales.

CANDID AND STRAIGHTFORWARD

Great businessmen typically possess a direct communication approach. They might have a great sense of humor, but it doesn't stop them from being straightforward about what they think and feel. Their candid communication style may sound harsh and unsympathetic, but this doesn't necessarily mean that they lack empathy. They want to eliminate any ambiguities and don't sugar-coat things. Also, the communication style results from their high expectations from themselves, their company, and their teams.

Sergio (center) receiving the Exporter of the Year 2018 Award from American Express. Global4PL was the first company to receive such an award.

CHAPTER ELEVEN

THINGS TO AVOID AS AN ENTREPRENEUR

For entrepreneurs, mental strength is more important than physical strength. Most people tend to define mental strength in terms of what entrepreneurs are capable of thinking and doing. However, mental strength is about things they "don't do." This section will discuss what strong entrepreneurs don't like to do. After going through them, try to shape your way of thinking and approach.

BELIEVING THAT ONE IDEA IS EVERYTHING

A common misconception is that success in entrepreneurship depends upon that one lucrative business idea. No doubt having an amazing business idea helps, but it has to be scalable and provide people with what they really need and would want. Plus, you may have a brilliant business idea, but without the capacity to execute the idea, that is, turn it into a living, viable, and breathing organization, it's deemed to fail. Thus, having a good business idea is only one piece of a large puzzle.

If Sergio had believed that one idea was everything, he would have never succeeded. He was willing to present his idea, watch it fail, then listen to his network to figure out how to fix it. Sometimes, an idea needs to be moderated or thrown out completely to make room for a plan that works. Be ready to let go if your first idea does not succeed.

REGRETTING THE PAST

While acknowledging your mistakes and learning from past experiences and failures certainly helps, overthinking your past disappointments or even fantasies of your golden business days only exhausts your mental energy. Instead of mourning on missed opportunities and regretting their past, top entrepreneurs invest their intellectual energy in optimizing their present and future. Entrepreneurs generally don't dwell over past mistakes, as this is wasted time that could be better used to make a positive decision about their current business. Acknowledge the lessons from the mistake, but let them go and focus on the future.

FEELING LIKE THE WORLD OWES YOU

Some individuals, who've had elite schooling and preparations believe that they deserve a salary, superior benefits, and of course, a comfortable life. That's not how entrepreneurs think. At every stage of life, they are prepared to work their way up and succeed on merits from the very beginning. Even those who are lucky enough to have funding understand the hard work that a business demands. Sometimes, nothing comes easy, but this doesn't bother the hardworking entrepreneur. He or she simply finds an innovative way to get what is needed, either through his or her own ideas or through the network that has been carefully crafted since the beginning.

NOT EMBRACING CHANGE

If you resist change for the fear of the unknown, you risk becoming stagnant and complacent, which greatly limits your entrepreneurial abilities. On the other hand, an environment of change and uncertainty energizes mentally strong businessmen and helps to bring out their best. Therefore, you should welcome and embrace change rather than run away from it. Figure out how the change will benefit your company, then fit it into your own business plan. This will help you not only succeed but might turn out to be exactly what you needed. Further, some change helps solve problems, so embrace it and find out how it can work for you.

HESITATING TO TAKE CALCULATED RISKS

Knowing the difference between calculated risks and absurd risks differs from one person to another, as every person views risk differently. However, generally speaking, the difference between a calculated risk and an absurd risk is based on the likelihood of an outcome based on the different factors affecting that decision. A calculated risk happens after the decision-maker has analyzed as many factors as possible, both known and unknown, that will affect the outcome. An absurd risk happens when decisions are ground in a sole factor, poor evaluation of all the outcomes, or a "gut feeling." When you are betting more than you can lose, you are operating on an absurd risk. If a risk seems absurd, bounce it off your network to find either solutions or ways to turn it into a calculated risk.

Jumping headlong into absurd risks is never recommended, but that doesn't mean you start fearing even the calculated risks. You will never be a successful entrepreneur if you aren't willing to take calculated risks. Thus, use your mental abilities to weigh the benefits and risks of business decisions, while assessing the potential downsides and chances of failure before taking any action.

TRYING TO SHAPE THINGS YOU CAN'T CONTROL

The top entrepreneurs never waste time on things they can't access or control, especially about other people. In fact, they won't even take the time to complain about aspects that are beyond their control. Complaining about these aspects, and trying to gain control over them, wastes valuable time that is better spent working with the aspects you can control. When faced with a problem, they'll focus on shaping their own attitude and response, and leverage tools and people they have control over.

REPEATING MISTAKES

Making the same decision over and over again and expecting improvements in results is a no-brainer. A sensible entrepreneur will learn from past mistakes and do their best to avoid them in the future. Likewise, they constantly assess the success of their decisions and keep looking for ways to improve them. Based on a study published in Forbes, self-reflection is among the rare strengths of successful entrepreneurs and executives.

Sergio learned this when his first business venture failed. He figured out the issue by talking to the college students and learning through collaboration that he needed to take another direction. This is a prime example of understanding that there was a mistake, working to find a solution, then applying the solution. Never be too arrogant to admit that you are still human and you will make some mistakes.

LOSING HOPE UPON FAILURE

After going through entrepreneurial life and early struggles, Sergio knows that failures are inevitable in the business world. Someone who gives up after one or two failures simply isn't strong enough. Recognize failure as a chance to improve. Every failure lets you know what doesn't work, so you'll be taking alternative actions next time. Failures help you get closer to your ultimate goals. Failure is only a failure if you don't learn from it.

EXPECTING IMMEDIATE RESULTS

Finally, you should never look for quick results. Entrepreneurship requires you to invest yourself and get ready for the long haul. You should certainly invest your time and energy in measured doses and celebrate every small milestone achieved, yet you should possess the "staying power." Genuine changes take time so you need to be patient to see results. It will take time before you even start generating leads, and even more time, perhaps months, to secure that first business deal, and break-even. It might take almost a year and a half before you get to see profits.

CHAPTER TWELVE

RECOMMENDATIONS TO PROSPECTIVE HIGH-TECH LATINO ENTREPRENEURS

Now that we know that Latinos are seriously underrepresented in the technological arena in Silicon Valley, efforts need to be taken by the Latino professionals themselves to make themselves heard.

1. First of all, own your identity as a Latino. No matter how challenging the situation is, don't ever forget who you are and where you came from. If you're proud of your identity and community, it might actually help you make the difference you want. Right from the education level, you bring different and rich perspectives to the table. As you bring your experiences into discussions, it will open up pathways and allow more voices to be heard. Owning your Latino identity makes you unique in your college or workplace and that can help you grow professionally.

2. Some Latinos tend to keep themselves, aloof from other Latinos, in an attempt to get surrounded by whites and be accepted in their circle. This doesn't do them any good. Latino professionals should maintain a strong connection

with the rest of the community. If you aren't convinced, attend one popular event such as the Association of Latino Professionals for America (ALPFA) Conference or the Silicon Valley Latino Leadership Summit (SVLLS) and you'll realize how much you've been missing. It's not merely about surrounding yourself with someone you can sympathize with, but also about having more diversity driving conversations. You'll come across some remarkable Latinos sharing amazing ideas and who are making real changes in their workplaces to promote a more inclusive environment.

One of the biggest issues is that Latino talent somehow remains hidden, while those of whites, Asians, and other communities continue to be highlighted. Therefore, Latinos must start discussing their skills, achievements, and accolades outside of the Latino community to grab attention and develop a valuable corporate network. HITEC (Latino Information Technology Executive Council) is a great organization that has done an excellent job showing off and promoting the Latino in Hitech.

3. Latino students and professionals should consider enrolling in STEM-related academic courses. These include the most demanded disciplines, namely science, technology, engineering, and mathematics. Latino parents should encourage their children to pursue their higher education within the same parameters.

4. It's not true that the Latino community lacks talent. There are many Latino entrepreneurs in Silicon Valley and around the country that have made it to the top. As the statistics show, our numbers are still low in the valley, however, we are ripe with talented individuals who are able to turn this

around. Do not get discouraged, and keep pushing forward in the valley. Help prove that we are talented, strong, successful people who deserve to be here as much as the white male.

Many Latino professionals are self-doubters. We need to trust ourselves and exhibit more confidence both in education and in the workplace. Many Latinos believe that they don't have a chance of getting accepted at the top US colleges, thus Latinos don't even apply in the first place. Closing the doors for yourself is no way of addressing the diversity challenges. Since applying is the only way to really be considered, all Latino students should apply to the top business schools.

Latino entrepreneurs that could not attend higher education shouldn't forget that is never too late to go back to school. We need to keep up to date and have the information and technological capabilities to be able to compete with the high-tech businesses of Silicon Valley. While we should certainly encourage our children to pursue higher education, Latino professionals should keep looking for opportunities to access education themselves. They must seek mentorship and sponsorship opportunities from reputable sources.

Hence, you have the talent, the raw material, and whatever it takes to establish high-tech giants. All that's required is to talk more about entrepreneurial success and believe in yourself.

CHAPTER THIRTEEN

COLLEGE AS A NETWORKING TOOL

While a college degree may not guarantee you success, it certainly provides a higher chance of succeeding for the would-be entrepreneurs. The college you enroll in, in particular, makes a big difference to define the degree of success.

College is a great first step into a successful entrepreneurial journey. If you or one of your kids makes it to the one of top schools, he or she will get a great education, but networking is what will open doors. While not enrolling at one of these schools won't put an end to your entrepreneurial dreams, entering them will certainly give you a boost in the career and convenience in raising investment. Let's explore the best colleges for would-be founders and entrepreneurs.

When it comes to hardcore entrepreneurship, the most active locations include Boston and the San Francisco Bay Area. Based on the insights shared by PitchBook, 4 colleges from those two locations have clearly proved themselves by producing the best entrepreneurs in the country.

Not surprisingly, Stanford University stays at the top of the list. Its proximity to venture capitalists and the most prolific high-tech companies make the key difference and have produced 1,178 entrepreneurs who've raised a round of venture capital. The University of California-Berkeley closely follows behind with 1,137 entrepreneurs that managed to raise investment funds. The college is situated 40 miles across the bay from Stanford.

One insight we obtained from the data is that the location and prestige of a college play the most significant role in building a large network of successful alumni founders. Even though the two colleges are pretty close in terms of the number of successful entrepreneurs, Stanford University's acceptance rate is much lower (5%) than that for UC-Berkeley (17%). UC-Berkeley enrolls around 29,000 undergraduates annually while Stanford's number hovers around only 7,000 undergraduates. This means that Stanford clearly stands out among the two by producing a higher number of talented entrepreneurs with fewer undergraduate enrollments.

The next three colleges on the list are both based in Boston. The Massachusetts Institute of Technology (MIT) comes in third with 941 alumni founders who successfully raised venture capital.

The fourth is Harvard University with 900 venture capital-backed entrepreneurs. Interestingly, the University of Pennsylvania ranks 5th with 838 alumni founders who raised investment funds.

You might be surprised to know that 5 of the top 10 colleges for producing entrepreneurs who secured venture capital investment are state-backed schools.

BEST COLLEGES FOR UNICORN FOUNDERS

Unicorns are privately owned companies valued at more than $1 billion. Among the most widely known Unicorns are Airbnb, Pinterest, Dropbox, Uber, and WeWork. PitchBook also used its data to rank colleges based on the number of Unicorn founders they produced.

Again, Stanford retains the top spot by producing 24 entrepreneurs launching 18 unicorns. Their combined investment adds up to $7.6 billion. Harvard, however, surpasses both UC-Berkeley and MIT in this list with 16 founders of 15 unicorns raising a total of $6.7 billion. MIT follows, producing 13 Unicorn founders of 9 Unicorns with a combined $3.8 billion investment.

UC-Berkeley takes the fourth spot with 10 entrepreneurs initiating 9 Unicorns with a $4.8 billion combined investment. The University of Illinois makes the 5th spot producing 8 founders of six Unicorns with a combined venture-capital backing of $3.6 billion. Out of the top 10 on the list, two of the universities are state universities.

Hence, enrolling at one of these universities will make things a lot easier. This, however, doesn't mean you just can't be a top businessman without graduating from one of them. There are many Latino and non-Latino entrepreneurs who made it to the top without even obtaining a college degree. Ultimately, it's all about consistently looking for opportunities and making the most out of them.

CHAPTER FOURTEEN

CONCLUSION

In conclusion, Sergio would like to tell all those young and no so young Latinos that we are strong and we need more entrepreneurs in Silicon Valley and in the country. The truth is that being an employee is great but we also need founders and business owners to create new opportunities for other Latinos and other minorities.

We as a minority can do better by creating companies without ceilings, creating companies where other people can look at us and say, I am welcome there. There are companies like Sergio's, where the CEO of the company is a minority just like him. So let's teach our kids from a young age that they should think about starting their business someday. If they create a business there will be no glass ceiling and they will provide opportunities to others to grow and reach as high as they can because there will be no unconscious bias against them. We need more entrepreneurs to create wealth that only founders of start-ups and business owners can generate and by the fault, generate generational wealth that will lift the whole community.

Sergio worked for corporate for 20 years, and it was a great experience. But since he started his own company, he has not worked a day for the last 17 years. When you love what you have created, a company that you have started with your own blood and sweat, it's not work. He loves what he does; it has provided him opportunities that he would have never been given in a corporate company, and he believes he has done the same to those who work for him.

If he can only get one Latino or minority to realize that he or she can also create a company and do what we all preach: no discrimination, diversity of thought, and skin are welcome, then he has done his job.

We need more Latino entrepreneurs in Silicon Valley and in the country. The truth is that being an employee is great but we also need founders and business owners to create new opportunities for Latinos and other minorities.